Come Clean!

Charles W. Keysor

CHARLES W. KEYSOR is founder and editor of "Good News" magazine, which serves as a "forum for scriptural Christianity within the United Methodist Church." He is also instructor in Christian journalism at Asbury College, Wilmore, Kentucky. Mr. Keysor was graduated in 1947 from Northwestern University, Medill School of Journalism, and has served as managing editor of "The Kiwanis Magazine" and "Together." Converted to Christ at the age of 35, he attended seminary and became a pastor. He has written Christian education adult curriculum, articles for various Christian and secular magazines, and another book, "Our Methodist Heritage" (David C. Cook, 1973).

VICTOR BOOKS

a division of SP Publications, Inc.
WHEATON. ILLINOIS 60187

Library of Congress Catalog Card Number: 76-3923
ISBN: 0-88207-732-5
© 1976 by SP Publications, Inc. World rights reserved
Printed in the United States of America

VICTOR BOOKS
A division of SP Publications, Inc.
P. O. Box 1825 • Wheaton, Ill. 60187

Contents

Foreword

Dr. Charles Keysor is a man of many talents. His gifts in communication arts, hymn writing, poetry, essays, and books endear him as a theologian and writer. His ability to interpret faithfully God's Word in this study-commentary on Psalm 51, his sensitivity to Christians' heartaches and spiritual struggles, his sense of humor, his awareness of the slings and arrows of denominational and parish life, his love for the out-of-doors, all are talents which God has given to and matured in Charles Keysor.

This study on guilt and repentance is an additional expression of his strengths. He sets aside the easy to tackle the difficult. He could have been content to write a commentary on Psalm 51, a case study of the problems of guilt, repentance, and forgiveness, or a confession out of his own experience. But he didn't. Because his commentary on Psalm 51 also illustrates real people and problems, we easily understand that what was true in biblical times is true now. And further, this book enjoys the benefit of having a trial run in a Sunday School class.

As a professional in the area of pastoral care and counseling, I am delighted—almost amazed, except I know Chuck—how chapters 1-4 follow the "proper" format in counseling: The person is *anxious,* feeling something is wrong; next, the problem is *identified;* it is then *located;* the person's *investment* in benefiting from the problem is explored (projections, playing games, etc.); and a *solution* (liberation) is proposed. This bifocal approach to actual human problems and God's Word in this volume follows closely the approach and goals in counseling.

The opening chapters draw us—as sinners—into the lives of Allan, Elaine, Mary, and Bill. We are one or more of these persons in thought, word, or deed. This sets the context and makes David's sin our size—not just king-size. Furthermore, both David's and our problems assume their cosmic dimensions; guilt is also soul-size. The author helps us see these truths and relationships without moralizing.

Finally, a personal word about the author. I have known Chuck for five years now and worked closely with him in the Good News movement in the United Methodist Church since my election to the Good News Board of Directors in 1973. We have shared in several major projects and decisions in the movement and they reveal two qualities which I have come to appreciate most in Chuck: the heart of a pastor and the spirit of the reformer. Quick to defend the truth of what evangelicals of the Wesleyan tradition call "scriptural Christianity," he is equally discerning and quick to convey the pastor's compassion to those of us who work closely with him in Good News, to Asbury College students, and to the wide world of Good News people who are very much his parishioners. His is the reformer's concern for theological purity in the name of scriptural truth and his life is also the pastor's soothing support and the compassionate touch or prayer.

I commend to you this man and this pastor's study of guilt and repentance from someone who has "come clean."

Paul A. Mickey
The Divinity School
Duke University

Preface

This book was born in a Sunday School class. For several years it has been my privilege and joy to teach an adult Bible study group in the First United Methodist Church of Wilmore, Kentucky. It is made up of Asbury Theological Seminary students and wives; also some Asbury College students, professors, and wives. Certainly this is a unique class.

About two years ago we began studying the Psalms. King David's matchless psalm of repentance, Psalm 51, was so rewarding that we lingered, and lingered, and lingered. What began as a glance at Psalm 51 ended five months later after 20 Sundays of fruitful exploration. This study carried us deeply into some basic Christian doctrines: original sin, Christ's atonement, sanctification, and many more.

We learned that genuine repentance goes much deeper than a casual "I'm sorry, God," flipped skyward. And it goes much deeper than the shallow, popular idea that God is an ever-tolerant, indulgent Father who will forgive and forgive, no matter what.

The deeper we delved into Psalm 51, the more I marveled at its relevance. It was, in fact, painfully real. Writing some 3,000 years ago, King David was bothered by guilt. So are we. And David was moved by the Holy Spirit to seek life-changing repentance. This is our need today.

Come Clean! is a result of these convictions. It was written in the hope that you, like our Sunday School class, might grow in faith; and that you might experience the clean heart and willing spirit for which King David prayed. This book is not a scholarly exegesis of Psalm 51, though the last two chapters do present a swift verse by verse survey. Nor have I attempted a systematic study of guilt and repentance in theology or in church history. Instead, I have written a sampler to awaken your interest, to inspire you to probe and to study the Bible. In the process, I pray that God may touch and heal your guilt, as He did King David's long ago.

As we read each day's news, or watch the evening television programs, we can see that Isaiah was prophetic of our day when he wrote, "All we like sheep have gone astray; we have turned every one to his own way"; and for this reason, "The Lord hath laid on Him [Christ] the iniquity of us all" (Isa. 53:6, KJV).

The quest for victory over human guilt leads always to Jesus Christ. He was speaking to our guilt when He invited us: "Come to Me, all you who are weary and burdened, and I will give you rest" (Matt. 11:28, NIV).

So be it!

1

Why Do You
Feel That Way?

Allan* couldn't understand it. Every time he looked
at her, he felt ashamed. At coffee break, in meetings, or when she just walked by his office on the
way to hers down the hall, he lowered his eyes.
He would rather walk barefoot over hot coals than
look into her eyes.

Why?

❋   ❋   ❋

She could hardly stand to be with her boss, a
kind and helpful older woman who was the depart-
ment supervisor. There had been no open power
struggle between them, but Elaine* felt uneasy and
uncomfortable whenever she talked with her boss.
Riding together with her to the company Christ-
mas party had been sheer torture.

In Elaine's mind, there was an invisible wall between them. She couldn't seem to get through the

*A pseudonym

wall, or around it. It may as well have been brick.
Why?

* * *

Mary* continually needled her husband. Her
sharp tongue always snipped him down, not only
when they were alone but also in the presence of
friends and family. Her eyebrow was often arched
in supercilious criticism of her mate. She had a
hundred subtle ways of trying to make him feel
like a dumb clod.

For more than 20 years she had kept it up.
Why?

* * *

Bill* knew there were times when he needed to
punish his children—for their own good and for
the sake of family sanity. But when the moment
came, he seemed paralyzed. So mother dished out
the scoldings, allowance restrictions, and spankings.
Dad just could not do it.

* * *

Beneath every person's quirks and foibles is a
layer of guilt. For some people, the layer is thick
and heavy. For others, it occupies a relatively small
part of their energies and attention. But *some* guilt
is the burden of everyone. The Bible claims that
"all have sinned and fall short of the glory of God"
(Rom. 3:23, NIV).

Guilt has a powerful, often-crippling effect upon
the way people understand themselves and their
relationships with others, and God.

Symptoms of guilt
Why was Allan ashamed to look at the woman

who occupied the office down the hall? Sometimes he had a fantasy about her—about them. In his imagination they ran away together . . . she leaving her family and he leaving his.

When he saw her in the hallway, or at coffee break, the fires of adultery kindled in his mind. He wondered, Did she know? Did she share his obscene fantasy?

The adultery which lurked in his mind triggered feelings of guilt, uncleanness, and betrayal of his own wife. So Allan always looked away.

Elaine?

She was smarter, quicker, and more perceptive than her boss. After a year on the job she began to feel (with some justification) that *she* deserved to be supervisor. Elaine never said anything, of course. But the injustice of it gnawed within her. If only her boss were a louse, she wouldn't feel so much like a traitor.

Elaine wondered if her boss knew how she felt. Did she suspect that at every opportunity Elaine complained about her to the company executives and their fellow employees?

Yes, Elaine thought, I am stabbing her in the back. I know it is wrong, but . . .

Bill?

Bill considered himself a failure as a father. His oldest child had had serious problems, and he, his wife, and their daughter had consulted for two years with a child psychologist. Gradually Bill had realized that he had been too harsh and rigid with the child. Overcompensating now, he feared repeating those mistakes with his younger children. So he did nothing; his wife became the "enforcer," carrying his responsibility.

This puzzled and annoyed her. Bill was strong and forceful till it came to putting down the paternal foot. Why was he so weak?

Mary?

Before marrying Tom, she had spent occasional Saturday nights with him in secluded motels. She had wanted his proposal so desperately! To please him, she had consented, though she knew that premarital sex was wrong.

After they were married, Mary's sense of shame remained. The guilt kindled on those Saturday night trysts made a poor foundation for the couple's marriage, home, and family.

Now Mary constantly criticized her husband, punishing him by humiliating him. It was her unconscious way of responding to the feeling of uncleanness she had lived with for so long.

Thousands of other examples could illustrate how deep-lying guilt profoundly affects people's lives and attitudes.

Guilt ranks high as a suspected spur to physical troubles.

Doctors know that many patients suffer from psychosomatic ailments—maladies for which no organic cause can be found. Emotions are widely recognized as the culprit.

Prominent psychoanalyst Dr. Samuel Silverman, reported *Time* (Sept. 30, 1974), thought that ". . . Lyndon Johnson's last heart attack, Robert Taft's terminal cancer, Joseph McCarthy's fatal liver ailment, and Richard Nixon's phlebitis all seem . . .

to have been triggered by the intense emotional stress of a traumatic event . . . ."

Dr. Silverman, *Time* reported, also recalled the case of a professor who developed serious sight problems, eventually becoming blind, after he had wished for the death of his father who also suffered eye ailments.

A man known to the author spent thousands of dollars for medicines, vitamins, and doctor bills. A physician who had known and treated him a long time said, "There's nothing organically wrong with _____. It is 100 percent emotional and psychological."

To listen to the ailing man was to hear a catalog of ills and grievances accumulated over many years. Hostilities and guilt, piled up layer upon layer, went all the way back to his childhood.

The author has made a number of canoe trips into the wilderness of Canada. On these trips my fellow canoists and I carry everything—clothing, food, tent, cooking utensils—in large canvas backpacks. When land separates lakes or rivers, all the gear, including the canoes, must be portaged up and down steep hills, across creeks, and through marshes (with mud sometimes waist deep). A portage of one and a half miles can seem endless. The weight of the backpacks and canoes gets heavier and heavier. Finally we must get rid of it or collapse.

This illustrates the reason for many a mental breakdown—the guilt load becomes unbearable. Emotional or physical collapse may result in extreme cases, but the usual symptoms of guilt are often less severe. Guilt shapes us as persons in hundreds of little-suspected ways. For example, a man is always overweight. He diets, loses weight; then he puts it back on again, diets, regains his lard once more. He wonders why he eats so compulsively.

Guilt is the likely villain. When he was very young, his mother was advised by the family physician to stuff her baby with food. (People used to think that the fattest babies were the healthiest.) Eager to be a good mother, morning, noon, and night, she pushed food into the tyke's mouth. When he cleaned his plate, he was overwhelmed with love and kisses. Failure to eat everything brought cold looks of disapproval, scoldings, and even spankings.

In those all-important first years, the boy learned that the way to win love and approval was to eat. Seeking acceptance, he established a pattern of compulsive eating—a pattern which rests upon a deep-down, inexpressible rightness about eating much and a sense of guilt for eating little. Thus the boy—now a man—avoids hangovers of childhood guilt and rejection by eating far more than is necessary. His built-in food-guilt complex frustrates every desire to remain thin.

In the Bible, 2 Samuel 11—12 relates the story of a man whose life is an object lesson about guilt and its remedy. One evening about 3,000 years ago David, King of ancient Israel, walked out onto the roof of his house (in those days roofs were flat and often used as porches). Looking down, he saw a beautiful young woman taking a bath. This was before indoor plumbing, and apparently Bathsheba thought she was secure on her secluded rooftop—not suspecting that the king himself might be watching her.

Seeing her, King David wanted her. As king, he had the power of life and death; his command could not be disobeyed. The king sent for her and then slept with her, though Bathsheba was the wife of one of his faithful soldiers.

A child was conceived, and David hoped to cover up his responsibility for the child by ordering Bathsheba's husband home from the battlefield. But Uriah refused to disobey a military code forbidding sexual relations during time of war. In a desperate effort, David ordered the commander of his army to assign Uriah to the front lines and to make sure that Uriah was killed. Uriah died, and when Bathsheba's period of mourning was over, David took her as his wife.

Israel's number one citizen had broken three of God's sacred laws. The Law of God, given in the Ten Commandments, issued by God through the prophet Moses, declared, "You shall not murder. . . . You shall not commit adultery. . . . You shall not covet your neighbor's wife . . ." (Ex. 20:13-14, 17).

David knew right from wrong, but he deliberately violated the deepest moral, ethical, and religious principles of his nation, his people, and his God.

For about a year David tried to live above his guilt. He pretended he had done no wrong, but deep down inside, guilt must have gnawed at his soul. Then, when Nathan confronted David with his sins, he was ready to confess them.

He wrote, "Have mercy upon me, O God . . . blot out my transgressions. Wash me thoroughly from mine iniquity and cleanse me from my sin. For I acknowledge my transgressions; and my sin is ever before me. . . . Hide thy face from my sins, and blot out all mine iniquities. . . . Cast me not away from Thy presence; and take not Thy Holy Spirit from me. . . . Deliver me from bloodguiltiness, O God" (Ps. 51:1-3, 9, 11, 14).

He felt unclean; he wanted to be made clean. He knew he was a lawbreaker, that punishment hung heavy over him, like a dangling sword.

Guilt. It grows and grows like weeds filling and choking a garden until all that was good and useful is killed by that which is ugly and poisonous.

"From the body of one guilty deed," wrote Wordsworth, "a thousand ghostly fears and haunting thoughts proceed."

Robert South, 17th century divine, once declared, "Guilt upon the conscience like rust upon iron, both defiles and consumes it, gnawing it and creeping into it, as that does which at last eats out the very heart and substance of the metal."

I'm not OK

In his book *Then Joy Breaks Through*, psychoanalyst Dr. George A. Benson tells the case history of a 19-year-old girl who was deeply disturbed and a great trial to her Christian parents. Becky had "kicked over the traces." She used heroin, speed, and other drugs; she was promiscuous. Her appearance was unkempt; she exploded in frequent rages and accusations.

More than a year of intimate counseling made it clear that Becky's problem was pervasive guilt—

> Guilt so strong it almost possessed her. She was momentarily relieved to have it out in the open, but she was terrified when she felt the destructive power of the guilt we had uncovered . . . Becky's life was devoted to the maintenance of an image which concealed her guilt . . .
>
> Her destructive behavior was not the cause of her guilt. Her behavior was a means by which she distracted herself and those who tried to help her from the pervasive guilt she felt for just being alive . . .
>
> Arrogance and hostility, theft and sexual promiscuity are often simply means by which people draw attention away from a malignant sense of guilt about their own person. . . ." [1]

Often we think that guilt is a feeling we have when we do something wrong. This is one kind of guilt; there is another, deeper kind of guilt. Dr. Benson describes it as "pervasive," flowing out of what we *are*. Just as a great spring pours forth water, so does the fountainhead of pervasive guilt pour forth a torrent of ugly thoughts and acts, subconsciously confirming what the guilty person feels at the core of his being: I am no good.

This deep inner sense of "I'm not OK" is a part of our basic human condition. The Bible tells us that the first people, Adam and Eve, disobeyed God in the Garden of Eden. Somehow this wrong choice by the first human pair brought sin into the

[1] George A. Benson, M.D., *Then Joy Breaks Through* (New York: Seabury Press, 1974), p. 26.

world, tainting every human. All are born with "a bent to sinning," as hymnwriter Charles Wesley put it. Unless we are somehow radically changed, our thoughts are evil and our actions are evil. We, like Adam and Eve, deserve God's wrath.

The Apostle Paul, writing under inspiration of the Holy Spirit, declared, "All have sinned and fall short of the glory of God" (Rom. 3:23, NIV). And centuries earlier King David had written: "The Lord has looked down from heaven upon the sons of men, to see if there are any who understand, who seek after God. They have all turned aside; together they have become corrupt; there is no one who does good, not even one" (Ps. 14:2-3).

Paul vividly describes the bitter fruits of sin: "Their talk is foul and filthy like the stench from an open grave. Their tongues are loaded with lies. Everything they say has in it the sting and poison of deadly snakes. Their mouths are full of cursing and bitterness. They are quick to kill, hating anyone who disagrees with them. Wherever they go they leave misery and trouble behind them, and they have never known what it is to feel secure or to enjoy God's blessing. They care nothing about God nor what He thinks of them" (Rom. 3:14-18, LB).

We are all stained and corroded with guilt for being less than God intends us to be. "All the world stands hushed and guilty before Almighty God" (Rom. 3:19, LB).

This is why you so often feel unclean—so far from God—so hostile toward members of your family—alienated from people at your shop or office—isolated in your church.

Yet we need to thank God for guilty feelings. Dr. Dennis F. Kinlaw, president of Asbury College, once observed, "The guilt, the pain, and the alienation of our world are grace gifts from God to remind us that the world in which we live is fallen. It would be dreadfully wrong for a wrong world to be right."

Guilt is that spiritual pain which reminds us of the mortal illness of our sin. Through our guilt, the Holy Spirit may drive us to the One who can heal and make us clean from all sin: Jesus Christ.

2

The Root
of the Problem

"Guilt is the source of sorrow," said Nicholas Rowe, English dramatist, long ago, "the avenging fiend, that follows us behind with whips and stings."

We saw previously that guilt can be the cause of many things you feel and do. It lurks, often unrecognized, behind many of your habits and quirks. As you seek to escape guilt's whisperings, it makes your life a bit of hell. It may cause you to doubt yourself, doubt God, and doubt other people. It may also cause you to project onto other people the uncleanness you feel about yourself.

The "jealous husband" imagines other men lusting after his wife, and her being unfaithful. He flies into a rage when he learns that a man from the local church stopped by to visit with her. Why? Because the husband himself has a roving eye or has had affairs with other women, and guilt for these actions lies heavy upon him. He quite naturally assumes that *all* men are as lecherous as he is. Thus every time his wife talks with another man, the jealous husband suspects that she is planning to overstep the marital boundaries. He projects onto other men the same adultery of which he stands guilty, either by act or imagination (Matt. 5:27-28).

A Symptom of Sin

A breaking or contemplated breaking of the Law of God sets off an inner alarm known as conscience. Like a burglar alarm sounding a warning that thieves have broken into a store at night, guilt sounds the warning when you break the Law of God. This conscience alarm often produces feelings of guilt.

Guilt may also be a result of sins by other people. An example is Becky, the tortured teenager mentioned in the previous chapter. Her enormous sense of guilt was complicated by the drugs she took, the boys she slept with, and the many things she deliberately did to anger her parents. But these were secondary sources of her guilt. The root cause of her guilt, says psychoanalyst Benson, was the sin of her parents.

Becky was born four months after they were married; she was probably the reason for their marriage. From the day of her birth Becky had been a perpetual reminder of her parents' early sex sin.

Unconsciously they communicated a feeling of loathing to their daughter. The sensitive child developed ingrained awareness that she was "no good"—as indeed her parents really felt, despite their words of love.

The sin of one generation is transmitted, with multiplied destructive guilt, to the next. The Scripture says, "I, the Lord your God, am a jealous God, visiting the iniquity of the fathers on the children, on the third and fourth generations of those who hate Me" (Ex. 20:5). The absolute holiness of God is contrary to all sin. And complex, imbedded, and multilayered guilt is one sign of our human depravity—of the chasm separating a fallen humanity from a God who is pure, perfect, and holy.

The alarm in a burglarized store must be turned off, or the irritating noise would drive anyone to distraction. When your conscience rings guilt day after day, year after year, it becomes a wailing, endless cacophany in the mind. The conscience alarm must be turned off, but only God, who turned it on in the first place, can do this.

Psychologists and psychiatrists can provide some help in overcoming guilt. They often help people recognize *why* they feel guilty. Psychology and psychiatry should be understood by Christians as possible first steps. God may use secular counselors to help you understand your guilt. This is diagnosis; the cure is something else.

God's Plan
Until you have a clear understanding of guilt's true origin, you are not ready to move ahead to claim the cure which God in His love and mercy has already provided.

God has a plan for all that He has made. In the

very beginning, after the world had been created, "God saw everything that He had made, and behold, it was very good" (Gen. 1:31). This included not only the land, the sea, and the creatures, but also the way His universe would operate.

This plan, shaped in the all-wise mind of God, included a clear standard of right and wrong in our relationship with God, our attitude toward ourselves and others. God revealed these moral principles through Moses on Mount Sinai.

Then God spoke all these words, saying,

I am the Lord your God, who brought you out of the land of Egypt, out of the house of slavery.

"You shall have no other gods before Me.

"You shall not make for yourself an idol, or any likeness of what is in heaven above or on the earth beneath or in the water under the earth.

"You shall not worship them or serve them; for I, the Lord your God, am a jealous God, visiting the iniquity of the fathers on the children, on the third and the fourth generations of those who hate Me,

but showing lovingkindness to thousands, to those who love Me and keep My commandments.

"You shall not take the name of the Lord your God in vain, for the Lord will not leave him unpunished who takes His name in vain.

"Remember the sabbath day, to keep it holy.

"Six days you shall labor and do all your work, but the seventh day is a sabbath of the Lord your God; in it you shall not do any work, you or your son or your daughter, your male or your female servant or your cattle or your sojourner who stays with you.

"For in six days the Lord made the heavens and the earth, the sea and all that is in them, and rested on the seventh day; therefore the Lord blessed the sabbath day and made it holy.

"Honor your father and your mother, that your days may be prolonged in the land which the Lord your God gives you.

"You shall not murder.

"You shall not commit adultery.

"You shall not steal.

"You shall not bear false witness against your neighbor.

"You shall not covet your neighbor's house; you shall not covet your neighbor's wife or his male servant or his female servant or his ox or his donkey or anything that belongs to your neighbor" (Ex. 20:1-17).

These commandments form the foundational understanding of divine concepts of right and wrong. Thus they are basic in any serious discussion of conscience from a biblical point of view. There is need to repeat them frequently as reminders to God's people. Especially is this true since many in the Church and the world today deny, ignore, or pervert the Commandments.

During His three years of public ministry, Jesus helped believers understand the full meaning of these commandments. He summarized His teachings embodied in the Sermon on the Mount (Matt. 5—7), this way: "You shall love the Lord your God with all your heart, and with all your soul, and with all your mind. This is the great and foremost commandment. And a second is like it; You shall love your neighbor as yourself. On these two commandments depend the whole Law and the Prophets" (Matt. 22:37-40).

God's commandments, given in Scripture, apply to all people of all times. Ignorance is no excuse—

when we are at cross-purposes with God, guilt results, for He created us to live by His enduring truth principles. The Bible is filled with God's instructions on these matters: The Sermon on the Mount and Romans 12 are especially valuable. When you obey God gladly, because you love Him and wish to please Him, you are in harmony with His will. But when you violate any of God's Laws, you are going "against the grain." You are like a person trying to swim up Niagara Falls. You are opposing the full wisdom, power, and love of the eternal God.

When this happens—and who can claim to be faultless in keeping God's law?—the conscience alarm bell sounds within you. This is the heavenly Father's way of protecting you. Guilt, making you miserable, is His way of warning you that something is wrong, that something must be changed before disobedience destroys you.

A man wakes up at night with a stabbing pain in his abdomen. He turns and groans, but the pain gets worse. So he wakes his wife and she calls the doctor.

"Get Jim right over to the hospital," the physician says, "it sounds as if he may have appendicitis."

An ambulance comes screaming to the front door. Soon Jim and his anxious wife are in the community hospital. Within an hour the doctor operates.

"It was a good thing you got your husband here when you did," the doctor explains to the wife after surgery. "His appendix was swollen with infection. Soon it would have burst and the infection would have spread throughout his abdominal cavity. That would have been extremely serious. But we caught it in time. Your husband will be OK."

Jim's terrible pain was a blessing in disguise. So it is with guilt. Like the pain of appendicitis, guilt warns that you have somehow violated God's immutable moral laws. Later we shall see that there is a remedy for your guilt as certainly as surgery was the remedy for Jim's infected appendix.

Two Case Histories

Two case histories from the Bible can help us understand both the danger and the potential value of guilt.

Ananias and his wife Sapphira (Acts 5) apparently were pillars of the Early Church in Jerusalem. The church was a close fellowship. "The congregation of those who believed were of one heart and soul; and not one of them claimed that anything belonging to him was his own; but all things were common property to them" (Acts 4:32). Living in this climate of "all for one and one for all," Ananias and Sapphira sold some property they owned and brought of the proceeds to the church. Perhaps the other believers thanked God that the couple were devoted entirely to Christ and had turned their backs on all worldly inclinations.

But Ananias and Sapphira were deceivers; they had secretly held back some of the money for themselves. They had lied to their Christian brothers and sisters. Worse, they had gone back on what seems to have been a promise to give all to God.

The alarm buzzer of guilt must have sounded deep in the souls of Ananias and Sapphira when they thought about fooling the church and cheating God. But they went ahead with their plans. The tragic results are recorded in Acts 5.

"Peter said, 'Ananias, why has Satan filled your heart to lie to the Holy Spirit, and to keep back some of the price of the land? While it remained unsold, did it not remain your own? And after it was sold, was it not under your control? Why is it that you have conceived this deed in your heart? You have not lied to men but to God'" (Acts 5:3-4). These words, given to Peter by the Holy Spirit, ripped away the mask to expose Ananias' inner self. The shock was such that "as he heard these words [of Peter], Ananias fell down and breathed his last; and great fear came upon all who heard of it" (5:5).

Soon afterward, Sapphira came in and also lied about the price of the land. She also died (Acts 5:7-10). Both had played hypocrite with the church and stolen what had been dedicated to the Lord.

The prophetic words of Peter may have been like a match tossed in a can of gasoline; the explosion of guilt ended their lives. Knowing the Lord, having experienced His redemption and received His Spirit by faith, both were His reborn children. They knew better, but they chose to sin against Him.

The actions of Ananias and Sapphira must have grieved God. His desire to rescue His children from the destruction merited by their sins applied to this misguided couple. In the Old Testament we see God's incredible patience with His chosen people —idolatrous, backsliding, blasphemously forgetful of the grace which He had already extended. He is the God whose steadfast love is so great that He goes the limit to rescue undeserving sinners from hell. So God did not simply assassinate the pair.

Guilt can kill. Remember Judas? He betrayed Jesus, and the guilt was so great that "he went away and hanged himself" (Matt. 27:5).

Perhaps Judas was the subject of 18th century poet Edward Young's wise admonition: "Let no man trust the first false step of guilt; it hangs upon a precipice, whose steep descent in lost perdition ends." From an awful precipice of guilt, Judas, Ananias, Sapphira, and many others have tumbled to destruction.

Peter himself once stood on the brink of guilt's disaster. His struggle shows how guilt may be the force which draws one eventually closer to the living God.

The shadow of Calvary loomed over Jesus and the disciples during their last evening together in the Upper Room. Jesus explained that His body would be broken and His blood shed, creating a new agreement through God which would save forever all who believe.

"You will all fall away because of Me this night," Jesus told them in the original communion meditation, "for it is written, 'I will strike down the shepherd, and the sheep of the flock will be scattered'" (Matt. 26:31).

Then brash Peter, the Rock, protested, "Even

though all may fall away because of You, I will never fall away" (26:33).

"Jesus said to him, 'Truly I say to you that this very night, before a cock crows, you shall deny Me three times'" (v. 34).

Peter replied, "Even if I must die with You, I will not deny You. All the disciples said the same thing too" (v. 35).

The story is familiar. Jesus was soon betrayed and taken captive by His enemies. The disciples scattered like a flock of sheep. Peter did, in fact, deny three times that he even knew Jesus. "And Peter remembered the word which Jesus had said, 'Before a cock crows, you will deny Me three times.' And [Peter] went out and wept bitterly" (26:75).

Can you imagine the guilt Peter felt at this moment? For three years he had known Jesus, walked with Him, listened to Him, had seen Him perform miracles and had watched while the Master was transfigured into mysterious glory. He, Peter, had been designated as the "rock." On this faith profession, Christ's Church would be built (Matt. 16:18). And Peter had boasted that *he* would remain faithful, even though all the other disciples betrayed the Lord.

Yet Peter denied Him *three times*.

Surely Peter's guilt must have been as great as Judas' and Ananias' and Sapphira's. But Peter somehow rose above his guilt. It did not destroy him; instead, it seems to have provided a much-needed humiliation so that the old braggadocio could die and a humble, more realistic Peter could be born.

The guilt that destroyed others became Peter's springboard to greater faith and usefulness. He became a keystone in God's plan for the New Age ushered in by the death and resurrection of Jesus Christ.

3

Let's Face It

Scripture does not record what went on inside Peter's mind when Jesus looked at him. But it is not hard for us to imagine. Even after walking many years in intimate closeness with Christ, we like Peter, still deny our Lord. Those who can find no such denial are blind, have obliterated the memory of unfaithfulness, or have never really known the grace of true salvation. "Indeed, there is not a righteous man on earth who continually does good and who never sins" (Ecc. 7:20).

Have you felt the twinge of shame, regret, and chagrin when you acted as if Christ had not died for you? Have you had the frightening realization flash like illuminating lightning across your mind: *I have failed my Lord?*

In such moments we are one with Peter. We share his guilt of betraying the One whom Paul

identified as "the Son of God, who loved me, and
delivered Himself up for me" (Gal. 2:20).

Leaving the Scene of Guilt

We wish we could know Peter's mind at his moment of denial, but the Bible simply says that he
"went out and wept bitterly" (Matt. 26:75). Even
this brief description tells us two important things
about winning the victory over guilt and shame.

First, Peter *went out.* He left the place of his
humiliation, the place where he had failed his
Lord, the courtyard outside the chambers of the
High Priest, Caiaphas. A cluster of curiosity seekers
had gathered there, knowing that inside, the
miracle-worker Jesus was being interrogated by
their religious leaders.

Some in the crowd had been among the mob
which arrested Jesus in the Garden of Gethsemane.
They and others were the hangers-on who surround
any place of power. Among these Peter had tried
to hide his identity, as he waited (inconspicuously,
he hoped!) to find out what would happen to his
Friend.

Strangely caught up in the crowd's godlessness,
he who knew so well the incarnate God was carried
away on the currents of betrayal. Like an under-
tow off an ocean beach, the crowd pulled Peter
away from Jesus into the sea of denial. It happened
so quickly—before Peter realized what he had
done, the rooster crowed. When guilt surged over
him like a tidal wave, *he went out.* He turned his
back on the Christ-mockers who had drawn the
"rock" into unfaithfulness.

The well-known Christian psychiatrist, Dr. Paul Tournier, identifies the source of Peter's anguish. "The only guilt is not to depend on God, and on God alone—'You shall have no other gods before me.'"[1]

Repent, in the biblical language, means "to turn around," "to walk in a new and opposite direction." Lewis Bookwalter said, "Repentance is turning away from sin to God. It is the grandest act of the human soul."[2] Repentance begins by "going out"—you quit the place where sin occurred, where your guilt was conceived. You leave and begin again in new surroundings. You turn over a new leaf; you make a fresh start.

When Saul of Tarsus was converted (Acts 9), he "went out" from among the Pharisees. He began preaching that Jesus of Nazareth, whose followers he had persecuted savagely, was in fact the Messiah of Israel, the fulfillment of every Jewish dream and longing. A radical turnabout!

Later, Paul expressed deep shame and sorrow because he had once persecuted the followers of Jesus, but he did not wallow in self-loathing. Instead, he "went out" to serve Jesus under power of the Holy Spirit.

Some sort of departure is always involved in making the correct response to guilt. Unless you make a radical turn, you have not really repented in the biblical sense.

---

[1] Paul Tournier, *Guilt and Grace* (New York: Harper and Row, 1958), p. 69.

[2] Lewis Bookwalter, *Repentance* (Dayton, Ohio: United Brethren Publishing House, 1902), p. xi.

Jesus said, "You will know them by their fruits" (Matt. 7:20). And James, the brother of Jesus, wrote, "Faith, if it has no works, is dead . . . . Just as the body without the spirit is dead, so also faith without works is dead" (James 2:17, 26). One "work," or evidence of true repentance is turning sharply away from sin and guilt.

Regretting Sin

Peter left the scene of his guilt; he also *wept bitterly*. This is the second important aspect of facing our guilt: there has to be a sincere, deep, bitter regret if guilt is to be taken away and cancelled.

But it is important that you are sorry about the right thing. Sorrow wrongly focused will have no influence upon your guilt. In fact, the wrong kind of sorrow can drive your guilt deeper and make it more complicated.

Suppose that two men have been caught stealing from their employer. There is publicity in the local newspaper and on television. Both men are disgraced in the eyes of their families, friends, and fellow-workers.

Both are sorry. But one experiences a selfish sorrow: he is sorry *that he got caught*. He is not sorry that he had betrayed his employer, that he had broken God's clear law, "You shall not steal," (Ex. 20:15), that he had done wrong. Rather his regret centered on the embarrassing publicity, the loss of his job, the blemish on his record as an executive.

The other man reacted differently. He regretted the same things that the other man did. But he carried another sorrow: he had failed his heavenly Father. He had offended not only his employer, friends, and family, but he had grieved God. He had let down the One who had loved him enough to sacrifice a beloved Son so that the businessman "should not perish, but have eternal life" (John 3:16).

This sorrow, a sadness known only by the godly when they slip downward into sin, was the hardest to bear. The other sorrow, a more superficial level of sadness, could be lived with. It would heal over; it could even be ignored. But the enormity of grieving God broke the second man's heart.

Godly sinners must feel sorrow as Peter did.

For betrayal committed against a loving God must produce sorrow. Otherwise you do not really love God, or know Him as your heavenly Father.

If you aren't sorrowful—if you *don't* quit the scene of your transgression, then you are not really repenting. Then you are only uncomfortable about being caught in wrongdoing, and that attitude is as far from real repentance as the east is from the west.

Peter faced his guilt frankly, and God forgave. He gave Peter another chance. Peter became one of the great leaders of the Early Church—thus fulfilling Jesus' intention to establish His Church upon the rock of Peter's faith.

A worthy foundation! It had been tempered in the fires of sin and been refined through godly repentance.

Judas, on the other hand, hanged himself. His guilt was fatal because he did not truly repent.

The difference between Peter and Judas is the

difference between the fallen world (Judas) and Christ's Church (Peter). The difference between Peter and Judas is the difference between faith and unbelief, between redemption and damnation, between liberation and bondage. And this same difference can be seen today in the lives of men and women as they deal with guilt, following either the pattern of Peter or of Judas. Regarding repentance, Bookwalter said:

> "Not everyone has sincerely repented but everyone knows that he *ought* to repent. And everyone who has a purpose, however vague and feeble, to become a better man knows that repentance is, on his part, the step out of sin into righteousness. He counts on taking it some day. So thoroughly has [repentance] become a part of the popular ethic, religious creed of our day that repentance is, in fact, the one chief, practical doctrine and feature of Christianity which commends it to the practical world." [3]

How your guilt is faced makes all the difference.

Facing Your Guilt

Paul Bern, an MGM motion picture producer, shot himself to death on September 5, 1932, only two months after he had married the glamorous Jean Harlow. *Parade* magazine recalled that his suicide note read: *"Dearest Dear: Unfortunately, this is the only way to make good the frightful wrong I have done you and to wipe out my abject humiliation. I love you. PAUL. PS: You understand that last night was only a comedy."*

---

[3] Bookwalter, *Repentance*, p. iv.

What happened?

Parade explained, ". . . Bern had a common-law wife, actress Dorothy Millette, confined to a sanitarium in Connecticut at the time he married Harlow. Dorothy Millette left the sanitarium and was about to visit Berne in Hollywood when he shot himself. He did not want to drag any of the parties into what he felt would become a messy bigamy suit."[4]

If *Parade* is correct in its analysis, the man was trapped. Like Judas, he chose the way of suicide even though God had provided the same way out which Peter found—the way which is available to *anyone* burdened with guilt.

A less spectacular example is this:

During a series of meetings with a group of pastors, a minister came and asked to see me privately. During our talk together he said, "I have something that's bothered me for years. When I was in seminary I cheated on my final Greek exam. When I took the test I accidentally omitted one section of the translation. Since I usually did well in class, my professor called me at home to see what had happened. Since he trusted me a lot, he said, 'I'll let you translate the passage to me over the phone right now.'

"I told him all right, excused myself for a moment, and got both my Greek New Testament and an English translation. Then I translated it over the phone. But I was actually reading from the English. I got an A in the class and graduated from the seminary with honors, but I can't look that professor in the eye to this day. Every time I think about it, I feel like a hypocrite. I've prayed and prayed about it, but nothing seems to change."

4 *Parade,* 17 August 1975, p. 2.

After talking over the situation, I suggested the only way to resolve the problem would be to telephone his professor and confess his cheating. He struggled with this for some minutes and finally said, "I just can't do it. What would he think of me?"

I've never seen this pastor since, but I imagine he's still haunted by his guilt. His refusal to confess his cheating left him a victim of self-punishment.[5]

Refusing to do the obvious thing meant that the minister really cared more about preserving his pastoral image than he cared about making amends for the wrong he had done.

Zaccheus

The minister's experience highlights an important aspect of honest repentance: it must take action to set right what is wrong. An example is Zaccheus, a man who had grown rich by cheating his customers. As a tax collector he could overcharge people as long as he delivered to the Romans the required tax.

Zaccheus' customers hated him for two reasons: his racket and his cooperation with the hated Romans. Zaccheus was an outcast, but he cared more about the size of his bank account than the scorn of people.

Then Jesus came by. There was a huge crowd, and because Zaccheus was "small in stature" he "climbed up into a sycamore tree in order to see [Jesus] for He was about to pass that way" (Luke 19:4). The meeting with Jesus changed Zaccheus.

---

5 Bill Counts and Bruce Narramore, *Guilt and Freedom* (Irvine, California: Harvest House, 1974), pp. 128-9.

The light of God's holiness illuminated his sordid life, revealing its filth like a 500-watt floodlight shows up the stains on a rug.

That evening when he entertained Jesus at his home, Zaccheus faced up to his sin and guilt with amazing directness. He said, "Behold, Lord, half of my possessions I will give to the poor, and if I have defrauded anyone of anything, I will give back four times as much" (Luke 19:8).

This illustrates Bookwalter's thought that true repentance requires that you "burn the bridges behind you."[6]

By desiring to right the wrongs he had done, Zaccheus made clear that he was serious about repenting. Think of the humiliation he would face in that little town! He would have to go from person to person explaining that he had cheated each one, that he was restoring four times the amount of what he had taken unjustly. Zaccheus had to say, "Please forgive me. I have sinned against you."

Was this more difficult than phoning a former professor and confessing, "I cheated in that exam 15 years ago"? Was it less difficult than facing a double marriage and repudiating the second wife?

Right Relationships

Jesus said to Zaccheus, "Today salvation has come to this house" (Luke 19:9). Salvation means wholeness. The runty tax collector was healed of his longstanding guilt feelings. Zaccheus moved from

---

[6] Bookwalter, *Repentance*, pp. 45, 50.

a *wrong* relationship with God into a *right* relationship. He graduated from a relationship of hostility with his customers into one of honesty and cleanness. But first he had to walk that uncomfortable corridor of repentance and confession.

This happens whenever there is true repentance on your part: right relationships are restored immediately between you and God and eventually between you and the people around you. Because Zaccheus, through repentance, was finally in harmony with God's will, he experienced that "peace of God which surpasses all comprehension" (Phil. 4:7), the blessed fruit of true repentance. There is no other way to be at peace with God, with others and with yourself.

Notice that the minister who had cheated in seminary knew no peace, even though he had prayed much about his sin. The peace he sought could not come until he had first shown sincere repentance, until he cared most of all about pleasing God, regardless of his reputation as a Christian leader and scholar.

The Danger of Unrepentance

Few human beings have faced the hour of death with such enormous reason for guilt as Adolf Eichmann, the 56-year-old Nazi convicted of having a central role in murdering six million Jews during World War II. A report of his execution in 1962 stated:

Just before he dropped through the gallows trapdoor, Eichmann told the witness in German, "After a short while, gentlemen, we shall all meet again. So is the fate of all men. I have lived believing in God and I die believing in God." In reaffirming belief, Eichmann used a term employed by Nazis who had left the church but still professed a belief in God.

Even in his last conversation, Eichmann expressed no admittance of guilt. In fact he professed an eerie calmness.

"You look very sad," Eichmann said to Hull as the final visit began two hours before his execution. "Why are you sad?"

Replied Pastor Hull: "We are sad because we know that your end is at hand. We kept warning you that it was near; now it has come. But if you'll repent we will not be sad. Have you changed any in your attitude since this morning? Are you sorry for what you have done? Are you ready to repent?"

Later, Pastor Hull reported, "[Eichmann] had denied Jesus Christ as the Son of God; he had claimed that he did not need a mediator between him and God. He said that the Bible was written by men, that it was but Jewish stories and fables and that he did not believe it was the Word of God." [7]

Like Adolf Eichmann, countless people try to "put on a good front." They pretend that they have not sinned, that no forgiveness is necessary. Unrepentant they live, scarred inwardly by their failure to face the truth. Unrepentant they die, leaving this world to face God solely on the basis of the record of what they have thought, said, and done in the span of years between birth and death.

---

[7] News item, by J. D. Douglas, *Christianity Today* June 22, 1962, pp. 32-33.

Those refusing to repent will be forever separated from God because they failed to follow God's wise plan for facing up to sin and guilt and dealing wih them in God's way. The unrepentant will experience a different eternity than Peter and Zaccheus know.

To be forever with God is the privilege reserved for those who face honestly sins and guilt NOW—who claim NOW the gracious promise of God. The Apostle John wrote, "My little children, I am writing these things to you that you may not sin. And if anyone sins, we have an Advocate with the Father, Jesus Christ the righteous; and He Himself is the propitiation [appeasement of God] for our sins; and not for ours only, but also for those of the whole world" (1 John 2:1-2).

Tournier aptly said, "The true guilt of men comes from the things with which they are reproached by God in their innermost hearts. Only they can discover what these things are. And they are usually very different from the things with which they are reproached by men."[8]

---

[8] Tournier, *Guilt and Grace*, p. 67.

4

Some Games People Play

A modern psychoanalyst said, "One must realize that guilty people falsify themselves in the hope of avoiding their guilt and the fear which guilt engenders."[1]

A World of Illusion

Nearly two thousand years ago, the Apostle John said, "If we refuse to admit that we are sinners, then we *live in a world of illusion* [author emphasis] and truth becomes a stranger to us. But if we freely admit that we have sinned, we find God utterly reliable and straightforward—He forgives our sins and makes us thoroughly clean from all that is evil. For if we take the attitude 'we have

---

[1] George A. Benson, *Then Joy Breaks Through* (New York: Seabury Press, 1972), p. 36.

not sinned,' we flatly deny God's diagnosis of our condition and cut ourselves off from what He has to say to us" (1 John 1:9-10, PH).

The "world of illusion" is common, even among Christians. Why do so few professing Christians "come clean" in confessing sin? Because the sin nature which we inherited from Adam includes the ability to rationalize. With amazing skill we deceive ourselves. We spin a web of clever reasons to explain away our sin, and to magnify the sins of others, thereby minimizing our own. Indeed, we often turn wrongs into virtue, so that what is really evil in God's sight actually seems good (Rom. 1:32).

One important work of the Holy Spirit is to penetrate our charade. In love and wisdom, God sends His Spirit to cut through our rationalizations. He cuts through human pretense like a surgeon. Thus the heavenly Father liberates us from the false comfort of our illusions. He takes away our "security blankets" and in exchange He gives His children the only true security: Himself.

A five-year-old boy once got angry at his mother. Considering her treatment unfair, the little boy stormed into his room and began packing his clothes into a paper bag. He would run away! He would show her!

Lovingly the mother watched him prepare to leave. She even helped by handing him a shirt and socks. Then she watched him stomp down the stairs, open the front door, and walk determinedly down the street.

Half an hour later the front doorbell rang.

She answered and there stood the runaway, be-draggled, tired, and with a serious expression on his face.

"Lady," he said, "somebody found your little boy."

Such exquisite pretention is not limited to children. People of all ages engage in games of pretending: games that salve hurt consciences; games intended to save face; games to ease some of the pain of living. Games which create that world of illusion as a hiding place from the discomfort of reality. Games which enable us to stop short of a full two-sided confession: "One side is the negative side. This expresses one's weakness, sin and need. The other is a positive side. This expresses one's faith." [2]

Dr. Eric Berne, the father of transactional analysis, analyzed 36 "games" in his bestseller *Games People Play*. The book describes only *some* of the things people do to evade reality.

God occupies no place in the world of pretending that Berne describes, but his book helps us understand people better. Berne's idea of games-playing can be easily transferred into church life, for Christians play their own sort of "games"—with God, with themselves, and with people in the church.

I Don't Know What to Do

Consider the cheating minister mentioned earlier.

---

[2] James G. Emerson, Jr., *The Dynamics of Forgiveness* (Philadelphia: Westminster Press, 1974), p. 17.

This man had studied the New Testament in its original language, Greek. He had been through three years of seminary. He had pastored a church; he had counseled many people with spiritual problems. But he played "games" with God when it came time for him to face up to an old sin.

His "game" might be identified as *But, Lord, I Don't Know What to Do about My Sin.* His "game" consisted of going through the motions of repeated prayer, thinking much and savoring, just a bit, the secret known to him alone: the "fast one" he pulled so long ago in seminary.

Common sense (let alone four years of college and three years of post-graduate study) points to a basic answer: Confess your sin to the person you sinned against.

And Scripture is also clear: "Confess so that you may be healed" (James 5:16). The immediate context of this verse is healing of physical ailments, but ailing relationships between people could also be included. If the guilty minister had done what Scripture clearly prescribes, his soul would have been healed of the rawness of his longstanding guilt.

Why did this minister play games with God? Evidently he played this game of *But, Lord, I Don't Know What to Do about My Sin* in order to avoid what was more important to him than a lie known to God: his reputation and status in the church.

Suppose he had phoned the seminary professor and confessed cheating 15 years earlier. Wouldn't this get around? Suppose that sometime this minister was being considered for the pastorate of a large, prestigious church. And suppose the pulpit-search committee contacted the seminary for references. Or suppose the minister became a candidate for superintendent or bishop. Suppose the Greek professor told somebody . . . and somebody told somebody else . . .

No, the risk was too great! So the minister decided confession was not possible. His career was more important than getting right with God. His game reveals the minister's true problem: idolatry. To consider anything more important than God, His kingdom, and His righteousness is to have an idol, a substitute deity, and this is the worst of all sins.

Yes, the games people play extend even into the very household of God, where we might expect people to be more honest. The games of church people often have an appearance of religion, but underneath they are as godless as anything in the world.

No Way Out

No Way Out was the game played by movie magnate Paul Bern, mentioned earlier. He was like the woman who started waxing her kitchen floor at one end and finished in a corner. There was no way out but to walk across the floor she had just waxed, ruining her work.

Apparently Bern had assumed that his first wife would be permanently institutionalized—dead, as far as their marriage was concerned. So he married the movie queen whom millions regarded as a sex symbol.

But when wife number one was released from the institution, Bern suddenly found himself with two wives. That was more of an embarrassment in 1932, when divorce was more socially unacceptable than it is today. Death seemed the only way out of this mess, so Paul Bern shot himself.

There is, in fact, no way out whenever we go against God's wise plan which governs our relationships with Him and with other people. One wife is God's plan; by breaking this divine law, Bern destroyed himself.

Yet his suicide was not necessary. Christ died long ago on Calvary to take the punishment for Bern's sins, and, in fact, the sins of the whole world (1 John 2:2). By faith the movie producer could have had Christ's cleansing blood applied to his sins. By faith he could have received God's Spirit, who would have guided him in untangling his messy personal life. By faith he could have found strength to do what Zaccheus did: get right with God and the people he had wronged.

Ignorant of or rejecting God's way, Bern took Satan's way, the way of suicide. Such can be the deadly consequences of games with guilt and repentance.

I Didn't Do Anything Wrong

A universal favorite game is called *I Didn't Do Anything Wrong.* Just pretend that you are innocent. Admit nothing. Apologize for nothing. Confess nothing.

This game, played by most people most of the time, is often played by whole nations and races.

Dr. Karl Menninger, well-known psychiatrist, makes this telling observation:

> For a time the guilt of a group aggressive action toward another group is painfully shared by all. But it passes quickly. Do the Campbells still deplore their massacre of the McDonalds in Glencoe? Have the people of Spain today any sense of guilt of the Inquisition? "Our overzealous ancestors," they sigh, if reminded.
>
> The people of France do no penance for their massacre of the Huguenots. "A sad blunder, which took from us some of the glamor and brains of France."
>
> The Germans may soon have forgotten Auschwitz and Buchenwald in spite of the pensions paid and the memorials erected. "Our misguided forbears!"
>
> The people of the United States have almost no sense of guilt for the enslavement of blacks, the mass murder of Indians, the dislodging of the Cherokees, the lynching of blacks, the exploitation of labor, or the theft of the Southwest from Mexico. "Those were rough, impetuous days," we explain. "So romantic! Picturesque but rugged. Our individualist ancestors had to win. Conquer the wilderness, break out the prairie and win the West." And dare we mention Hiroshima?[3]

Displaced Blame

You Made Me Do It! is the game that destroyed the marriage of one couple.[4] Paula was divorced after 12 years of marriage to a compulsive alcoholic. She had two children and a good job when

---

[3] Karl Menninger, *Whatever Became of Sin?* (New York: Hawthorn Books, 1973), pp. 98-99.

[4] *Philadelphia Inquirer*, 2 March 1975.

she met Jim, father of five children, married, and 18 years her senior. Eventually Jim got a divorce, left his family, and married Paula.

"What followed," said Paula, "was a wonderful honeymoon and then one year and 51 weeks of hell. I think he really hates himself—because he feels so guilty about leaving his children. And he's taking his hatred out on me. He doesn't treat me like a queen bee anymore; he treats me like dirt under his feet."

Naturally.

If ours is a moral universe, could a woman desert her sick husband and could a man desert his family and then could they expect to find happiness in a second marriage? No, for God has ordained marriage of *one* man and *one* woman. Only death can dissolve that relationship.

By her divorce, Paula violated the plan of God. By his divorce (compounded by the abandonment of his five children), Jim too violated God's Law. Guilt was the inevitable fruit of their multiple disobedience. God's blessing was withheld from two people who selfishly tried to secure their own happiness at the expense of others. These kinds of plans seldom, if ever, work out.

"It's as if he blames *me*—holds *me* responsible for causing him to leave his children," Paula said. "He hates himself and he's trying to pull me down to his level."

Jim had left his wife and children by his own choice. Paula was only the trigger—the excuse which he used to escape from the heavy responsibility that rests upon the shoulders of fathers of big families.

But Jim did not accept responsibility for what he had done. Instead he played the game *You Made Me Do It!* He was making Paula responsible, shifting his own deep guilt to her.

Holier Than Thou

The great game-players of the Bible were the scribes and Pharisees, the most religious people among the Jews. They were the ones who claimed to understand the Scriptures. They were famous for praying long and pious prayers. And they were scrupulous about giving God one-tenth of everything—even down to the seeds they harvested from their gardens.

But Jesus exposed their games. That is why they hated Him so. He said:

They [the Pharisees] tie up heavy loads, and lay them on men's shoulders; but they themselves are unwilling to move them with so much as a finger!

But they do all their deeds to be noticed by men; for they broaden their phylacteries and lengthen the tassels of their garments.

And they love the place of honor at banquets, and the chief seats in the synagogues, and respectful greetings in the market places, and being called by men, "Rabbi."

Woe to you, scribes and Pharisees, hypocrites, because you shut off the kingdom of heaven from men; for you do not enter in yourselves, nor do you allow those who are entering to go in.

Woe to you, scribes and Pharisees, hypocrites!

For you clean the outside of the cup and of the dish,
but inside they are full of robbery and self-indulgence.
You blind Pharisee, first clean the inside of the cup
and of the dish, so that the outside of it may become
clean also.

Woe to you, scribes and Pharisees, hypocrites! For
you are like whitewashed tombs which on the outside appear beautiful, but inside they are full of dead
men's bones and all uncleanness" (Matt. 23:4-7, 13,
25-27).

The Pharisee's game can be called *I Am Holier
than You.* They went through elaborate rituals to
demonstrate their spiritual superiority. But inside,
their hearts had no devotion to match their religious
play-acting. Instead, they were selfish, jealous,
greedy, and murderous—just like the people who
made no show of religion. If their outward show
of religion had been matched by inward love for
God and neighbor, then the Pharisees would have
been genuine. And God would have rejoiced in
their honesty.

But Jesus condemned them with scorching meta-
phors: "You blind guides, who strain out a gnat
and swallow a camel" (Matt. 23:24); "You serpents,
you brood of vipers, how shall you escape the
sentence of hell?" (Matt. 23:33)

Jesus had no scalding words for the woman
caught committing adultery (John 8:3-11), or for
the criminal who died beside Him on Calvary
(Luke 23:40-43). He reserved His harshest words
for people who *pretended* to be better than others
—but were actually unholy down inside, where
God alone could see.

Games Church Members Play

Why do people play the game of pretending to be holy, religious, and good?

One reason may be the need to cover the guilt they feel because they know they are really less than what God wants them to be. They believe that by play-acting they can fool God as well as their neighbors. They may carry large Bibles to church; they may attend every church service and meeting. They may witness; they may tithe; they may lead in public prayer. But they forget that "God sees not as man sees, for man looks at the outward appearance, but the Lord looks at the heart" (1 Sam. 16:7). They forget that "the ways of a man are before the eyes of the Lord, and He watches all his paths" (Prov. 5:21).

It is easy for us to diagnose the games played by the Pharisees; it may be harder to recognize those same guilt-induced games which many church members play. Consider:

• *The businessman* He gives liberally to his church—to compensate (in his mind, at least) for shady business deals and for cheating the people of his community by taking advantage of publicized scarcities to raise the already high prices of his products.

• *The housewife* She hides in the church kitchen, dutifully washing pots and cooking macaroni for church suppers. "She is really dedicated," people say of her ceaseless labors.

But actually, she is running from God. She feels that if she works in the church kitchen, God will somehow overlook her failures to pray, to love Him

with all her heart, to show love to her neighbors
and children.

She has discovered that people who wash dishes
and clean up after church suppers are excused from
hearing the preaching and witnessing that goes on
after eating. So the woman slaving in the kitchen
may be a female Jonah, running away from the
Lord—even as she gives the appearance of being
a devoted churchwoman. Her faithful service may
be a fruitless act of atonement for her guilt.

• *The youth* He hears God calling him to full-
time Christian service. But he has a car that demands all his time. He has buddies to run with,
and they never go to church. And he has a girl-
friend who thinks church is a drag.

So he is pulled steadily away from God, away
from worship, away from prayer—and away from
God's call upon his life. The Voice still speaks but
he pretends not to hear. And this lays the foundation of guilt that will remain as long as he, like
Jonah, continues to evade God's claim on his life.

Many people active in the church feel deep
guilt about ignoring or suppressing God's calling.
The evader often tries to "make up" for it by being
active on committees, teaching a Sunday school
class, and becoming a "pillar of the church." But
the true motive is neither love for God nor yearning to be in God's house with God's people. Instead, the real reason may be a lifetime of guilt
and the desire to atone for it by activity in and
around the church.

I once talked with a man who was very religious.
He belonged to a very conservative denomination

—the kind in which people argue to the point of schism over detailed theories of Christ's second coming. He was orthodox to the core, and he could quote the right Scripture at the drop of a suggestion. He appeared to be the perfect Christian.

Yet all was not well underneath the veneer. He had deep feelings of insecurity. Lacking a formal education, he struggled with a crippling sense of his own unworthiness. In many ways he was still a child. He had never worked through childhood conflicts with his parents, brothers and sisters, and other authority figures. So underneath his religious exterior seethed a volcano of self-doubt, guilt, and frustration.

I tried to help him face his inner turmoil. But he was skillful at using religion as a shield, as a hiding place. He diverted my attention from his problem to Scripture verses and all kinds of questions. Which theory of Christ's atonement was correct? Would Christ return before or after the great tribulation? What "signs of the times" had appeared lately to herald the soon return of Jesus Christ?

His questions concerning these arguments were valid. But God does not intend that such matters should be used by His children to escape daily reality or as a mechanism to suppress or bypass the painful and frightening feelings which often tear at our vitals and cripple us as human beings.

The most sacred and holy things can be twisted into games which serve Satan instead of the living God. This brings us back to Benson's statement at the beginning of this chapter: "One must realize that guilty people falsify themselves in the hope of avoiding their guilt and the fear which guilt engenders."

Intelligent Christians need to recognize the world of illusion which unconfessed guilt often breeds. We need to realize how easily we slip into unreality when it comes to our own guilt.

But God, in His love, has provided a way to set our feet on solid ground, a way by which even the weakest person can triumph over the world of illusion and the suicidal games which so often seem a passport to happiness but are, in reality, a ticket to oblivion.

5

We Can Overcome!

Once I took a canoe trip with two of my children into the wilderness of the Quetico Provincial Park in Ontario, Canada—there were no stores, no roads, no motels.

One night a storm blew our canoe away from the island where we had set up camp. We were helpless; we could do nothing to rescue ourselves. We could only wait until help came from somewhere else.

On the evening of the fifth day Canadian Rangers circled our prison island in a seaplane and landed. The plane taxied up to our beach, and we quickly packed our gear and climbed on board. One hour later we were back in civilization.

God and Our Guilt
Our adventure is a parable of God and our guilt.

Each person is marooned in guilt because he has "a bent to sinning," because there are so many wrong things we have done and so many right things we have failed to do. Our guilt affects us in many ways—sometimes to the point of destroying us.

By ourselves we are helpless prisoners of guilt. Just as three people stranded on a wilderness island could not rescue themselves, so each human being is powerless to save himself. Rescue must come from beyond ourselves.

The Canadian Rangers, flying a seaplane, rescued the marooned campers from the lonely island in Ontario. But the One who alone can rescue us from our guilt is the living God, the Holy One of Israel. No one else has the sheer love, the power, and the ability to do for us what we cannot do for ourselves.

Our Deliverer

What has our rescuer done?

First, God made known His perfect Law through the Bible. His Law teaches His children what is wrong, what is right, and what is best for us. It points the way to life that is abundant, fruitful, and filled with meaning. It points out the path of obedience which leads to the blessing of eternity with God.

God set a moral current, like the current in a mighty river, flowing in His universe. People who persist in swimming against this current can be frustrated and even destroyed. God's Law tells us which way this moral current flows. It flows first to God: "You shall love the Lord your God with all your heart, and with all your soul, and with all your mind" (Matt. 22:37). Then it flows to other people: "You shall love your neighbor as yourself" (Lev. 19:18; Matt. 22:39). Love for one's neighbor manifests itself through obedience to God's commands prohibiting murder, stealing, adultery, and covetousness (Ex. 20:13-17).

But God's Law has another purpose: "The Law has become our tutor to lead us to Christ, that we may be justified by faith" (Gal. 3:24). The Law, found in the Pentateuch, points to the One whom God would send to provide the only true solution to human sin and guilt.

Our Deliverer is Jesus of Nazareth, the Christ, the Messiah, the Promised One for whom true Jews had been watching and waiting.

Guilt and Our Deliverance

About 700 years before Jesus' birth in the manger at Bethlehem, the Prophet Isaiah foretold what was to happen—how this Christ, the suffering Servant, would take away the guilt of all who would accept His sacrifice. This is the most important prophecy of the entire Old Testament, because it explains how God has already arranged to rescue you from guilt and sin. The prophet Isaiah said, "Surely our griefs, He Himself bore, and our sorrows He carried" (53:4). Jesus might be compared to a friend who meets you at the airport and says, "Let me carry your luggage; it is too heavy for you." Love causes Him to be our Porter, carrying what we ourselves cannot carry. Love for you causes Him to carry your heavy baggage of guilt, shame, and meaninglessness.

Sin—Stealing from God

A great burden was carried by the businessman who turned his back when God called him as a boy. All through life he sensed that he had chosen second best, that he had run away from God. No matter how great his success in business, guilt festered in his heart. Persistent guilt was the burden carried by the preacher who would not confess his cheating.

Jesus will carry these burdens of guilt and every other burden. You can cast "all your anxiety upon Him, because He cares for you" (1 Peter 5:7).

Isaiah further described our Deliverer: "He was pierced through for our transgressions, He was crushed for our iniquities" (53:5).

No one is sinless—which means all have guilt. All have fallen far short of the perfection for which God made us. Jesus made this very clear: "You [disciples] are to be perfect, as your heavenly Father is perfect" (Matt. 5:48). God Himself is our standard. Anything less perfect than He is falls short of the mark, and this is sin. Paul said, "All have sinned and fall short of the glory of God" (Rom 3:23).

For this reason all humanity stands under God's indictment. All deserve punishment, for each sin amounts to stealing from God—a diminishment of His will and plan. That is why every sin is ultimately a sin against God Himself. King David, who had committed adultery with Bathsheba, had killed her husband, and then deceived his people, said in repentance, "Against Thee, Thee only, I have sinned" (Ps. 51:4).

Ananias and Sapphira stole from God money which they had dedicated to Him. They died suddenly, perhaps overwhelmed with guilt for what they had done. (See Acts 5:1-10.)

The Consequences of Sin

What might be suitable punishment for stealing from God a life that rightfully belongs to Him? What might be fair punishment for ignoring His love, and acting as if all your blessings come from your effort rather than His kindness?

Punishment for sin can be short- or long-term, or both. Short-term guilt may be sent by God to warn you that you have cheated Him somehow. Because He loves you, He hopes guilt will awaken you and cause you to turn from sin before it is too late. The consequences of sin can be great, because:

> One sin destroys much good, and terrible evils sprung out of this iniquity [of King David]. True, David received forgiveness, but forgiveness does not arrest the consequences of deeds which we have committed. It does not prevent the operation of the natural law whereby sin works ever toward misery and retribution. It restricts the punishment of iniquity, in the case of the forgiven one, to the present life. But within the limit the consequences of sin, even to a child of God, as David was, are often very dreadful. . . .

Recall for a moment . . . the consequences of David's sins . . . He caused the death of Uriah, and the sword departed not from his house all his after-days. He was guilty of impurity, and his son Amnon bettered the example which his father set: [he raped his half-sister]. Absalom [another son of David] committed fratricide; he rebelled against the Lord and against David. And all this even though [David's] sin had been forgiven! [1]

Yet, "The Lord . . . is patient toward you, not wishing for any to perish but for all to come to repentance" (2 Peter 3:9)

To "perish forever, eternally in hell, is the frightful long-term divine punishment. It is reserved for people who refuse, during their earthly lives, to stop sinning, to repent honestly, to accept God's forgiveness, and to obey God.

God, respecting each person's free will, says, in effect, to the unrepentant: "I have wanted you to be rescued! I have made the offer, but you have refused it. So I grant you your wish. You will remain forever as you have chosen to be—an eternal prisoner of your sins and guilt. The Great Liberation time is gone for you. By your disobedience, by your refusal to walk in My pathway, you will be forever separated from Me. I, who would have been your God, will bother you no more. Now Satan, your true father, will welcome you into his kingdom, where the fire burns forever, and where the acids of regret and remorse never end. Live forever as you chose to live: under Satan's rule."

To be cut off from God! To miss out on His forgiveness! To continue on forever the miserable way

[1] William H. Taylor, *David, King of Israel* (New York: Harper, 1876), pp. 275-6, 281.

you are! Knowing everyone faces these terrors of eternity without God, the true Church has zealously sought out sinners to extend to them Jesus' invitation to redemption.

H. A. Ironside wrote, "Everywhere the apostles went they called upon men to face their sins. [This meant] to face the question of their helplessness, yet their responsibility to God—to face Christ as the one, all-sufficient Saviour, and thus by trusting Him to obtain remission of sins and justification from all things." [2]

Jesus was the suffering Servant. As Isaiah prophesied, Jesus took on Himself the punishment for sin each person deserved. His death, recorded in Matthew 27, Mark 15, Luke 23, and John 19, had been predicted by Isaiah: "He was pierced through [with nails and a spear] for our transgressions, He was crushed [with the agony of dying] for our iniquities. And the chastening for our well-being fell upon Him, and by His scourging we are healed. . . . The Lord has caused the iniquity of us all to fall on Him. . . . He Himself bore the sin of many, and interceded for the transgressors" (Isa. 53:5-6, 12).

No one can fully understand or explain the great miracle of Christ's dying for sinners. It is only God's grace—His unmerited favor. One of Jesus' disciples wrote: "God so loved the world, that He gave His only begotten Son, that whoever believes in Him should not perish, but have eternal life.

---

[2] H. A. Ironside, *Except Ye Repent* (Grand Rapids: Zondervan Publishing House, 1972), p. 15.

For God did not send the Son into the world to judge the world; but that the world should be saved through Him" (John 3:16-17).

Justification

The miracle of justification, or coming into a right relationship with God, happened the instant the Holy Spirit led you to say, "I believe that Jesus is indeed my Saviour. I believe that He did die for me. I believe that now, because of His death, my sins are canceled out. I believe that God remembers my sins no more, because His beloved Son died for me, a sinner, lost, wretched and deserving hell."

When this "saving faith" is born, a two-fold miracle happens.

First, the believer is forgiven of the debt owed God for every sin, every wrong thought, every impure word, every mixed motive, every wrong desire.

It is as if a rich uncle paid off the mortgage on your home. The bank president would call you and say, "I have wonderful news for you! Your mortgage has been paid in full. Your debt to us is canceled."

By one great miracle, the atoning death of Jesus Christ, God has taken away the ground for all your past, present, and future guilt. This fact is the "good news" of the Gospel, the heart of true Christianity. Realizing this, making this grand liberation the keystone of your life, is what it means to be a Christian. One so freed from guilt can say joyfully:

"So now, since we have been made right in God's sight by faith in His promises, we can have real peace with Him because of what Jesus Christ our Lord has done for us. For because of our faith, He has brought us into this place of highest privilege where we now stand, and we confidently and joyfully look forward to actually becoming all that God has had in mind for us to be" (Rom. 5:1-2, LB).

"So there is now no condemnation awaiting those who belong to Christ Jesus. For the power of the life-giving-Spirit—and this power is mine through Christ Jesus—has freed me from the vicious circle of sin and death" (Rom. 8:1-2, LB).

The second part of the miracle of "saving faith" is: Jesus Himself comes to live with you and in you! He can do this now because He is risen from the dead. No longer is He confined, as we are, to being in only one place at one time. Now He is, literally, with all who love Him. He told His disciples after His resurrection, "Lo, I am with you always, even to the end of the age" (Matt. 28:20).

The writer of Hebrews also said, "For He Himself [Christ] has said, 'I will never desert you, nor will I ever forsake you'" (Heb. 13:5).

The Apostle Paul, who was one of the most effective and articulate followers of Jesus, described it this way: "The mystery which has been hidden from the past ages and generations; but has now been manifested to His saints, to whom God willed to make known what is the riches of the glory of this mystery among the Gentiles, which is Christ in you, the hope of glory" (Col. 1:26-27).

Only because he was aware of Christ's constant presence could Paul boast, "I can do all things through Him who strengthens me" (Phil. 4:13). Christ, living in Paul, explains why Paul was one of the greatest Christians who ever lived.

The Christian life is sometimes described as "sanctification," or "growing in grace," or "going on to perfection." This means Christ Himself triumphing over the believer's human frailty, Christ turning human weakness into glory for God.

It is an accelerating process: the more you open yourself to Christ, the more He will fill you with His attributes—"love, joy, peace, patience, kindness, goodness, faithfulness, gentleness, self-control" (Gal. 5:22-23). As these qualities of Christ are reproduced in you, they displace your guilt. As you are increasingly filled with wonder, love, and praise for God, there will be less and less room left for morbid fixations on past sins, mistakes, and foolishness.

Sin and Grace

A teen-age boy once disobeyed his father. As was the family custom in those days, father and son went out back to the woodshed. But instead of picking up a whip, the man said, "Son, take that hammer over there and drive a nail in that piece of wood."

The boy did as he was told.

"Now pull out the nail," his father directed.

The boy did so.

"Now pull out the hole."

Our sins leave scars, many of which cannot be

erased, even though the sting of sin disappears. Your guilt is healed through the cross, and by the presence of Christ living His life through you, but the scar tissues remain. They constitute, for the faithful, a sobering reminder of weakness and of the mercy of God.

Becoming mature as a Christian brings to light many sins which you did not recognize before. And with each such discovery comes fresh need for the believer to draw upon God's resources to deal with that freshly uncovered guilt.

One man lived many years before he came to know Christ as his Saviour. Proudly he called himself a self-made man. Then Christ entered his life. He began to grow in faith, and the Holy Spirit opened his eyes to an important truth: All his possessions and business achievement had been made possible by God.

This realization came as a shock. The rug was pulled out from beneath his pride, and he suddenly became aware of his gross ingratitude growing out of his amazing arrogance toward God. But God had loved him in spite of his blindness; God had blessed him anyway.

Like a tidal wave, guilt overwhelmed him. And like Peter the apostle, the new Christian wept over his sin. Then the Holy Spirit spoke to him: *My son, I'm glad you have learned this lesson. Never forget that My love is not based on your worthiness but upon the fact that it is My nature to love and redeem.*

Great Bible teacher Harry A. Ironside said this about the realization of guilt:

It was when Mephibosheth realized the kindness of God as shown by David that he cried out, "What is thy servant, that thou shouldst look upon such a dead dog as I am?" (2 Sam. 9:8) And it is the soul's apprehension of grace which leads to ever lower thoughts of self and higher thoughts of Christ. And so the work of repentance is deepened daily in the believer's heart. . . . The very first evidence of awakening grace is dissatisfaction with one's self and self-effort and a longing for deliverance from chains that have bound the soul.

To own frankly that I am lost and guilty is the prelude to life and peace. It is not a question of a certain depth of grief and sorrow, but simply the recognition and acknowledgement of need that leads one to turn to Christ for refuge. None can perish who put their trust in Him. His grace superabounds above all our sin, and His expiatory work on the cross is so infinitely precious to God that it fully meets all our uncleanness and guilt.[3]

Martin Luther, father of the Protestant Reformation, taught that the proper Christian life is one continuing act of repentance.

How true that is. The more you grow in Christ, the more you come face to face with the distance between you and Him. Thus a maturing Christian is often on his knees praying, "Lord, be merciful to me a sinner."

God always hears such a prayer. It comes from the heart, and out of His heart—of limitless love comes His reply, *Rise up and walk! Your faith has healed you of remorse, guilt, and belittling. Grace caused your heart to fear. Now that same amazing grace causes your fears to be relieved.*

---

[3] Ironside, *Except Ye Repent,* pp. 16-17.

6

Barriers
to Forgiveness

Dr. Karl Menninger's book *What Ever Became of Sin?* begins with this anecdote:

On a sunny day in September 1972, a stern-faced plainly dressed man could be seen standing still on a street corner in the busy Chicago Loop. As pedestrians hurried by on their way to lunch or business, he would solemnly lift his right arm, and pointing to the person nearest him, intone loudly the single word, *"GUILTY!"*

Then, without any change of expression, he would resume his stiff stance for a few moments before repeating the gesture. Then, again, the inexorable raising of his arm, the pointing, and the solemn pronouncing of the one word, *"GUILTY!"*

The effect of this strange . . . pantomime on the passing strangers was extraordinary, almost eerie. They would stare at him, hesitate, look away, look at each other, and then at him again; then hurriedly continue on their ways.

One man, turning to another who was my informant exclaimed, "But how did *he* know?" [1]

This modern-day Chicago prophet had his own reasons for acting like Isaiah and Jeremiah. Either knowingly or by accident he touched upon one of the realities of human nature: Everyone stands guilty before God.

The annoying persistence of guilt creates serious problems for even many Christians. They continue to *feel* guilty even though they know *in their minds* that Christ has made full atonement for their sins, that through Christ, God has forgiven each sin and remembers past transgressions no more.

The assurance of forgiveness has not left their minds to penetrate their feelings. No matter what the Bible says—the preacher says—the hymns say —or the liturgy of Communion declares about forgiveness through the atoning blood of Christ, still their feelings accuse them—like the man on the Chicago street corner—crying, *"Guilty! Guilty! Guilty!"*

The Unforgivable Sin

As a pastor I spent many hours counseling a young man who was deeply troubled. He could not hold a job. Often he slept most of the day—a sure sign of deep emotional turmoil. His attempts to be friendly with other people were clumsy or downright repelling.

In counseling, the young man's disorientation became evident. Delving deeper into his problem

[1] Menninger, pp. 1-2.

(like peeling the layers of an onion) we finally got to one major source of his trouble.

In a fit of anger, he had once cursed the Holy Spirit. This, he was certain, meant that he could never be forgiven. The young man had a surprising knowledge of the Bible. He quoted fervently the verse, "Whoever blasphemes against the Holy Spirit never has forgiveness, but is guilty of an eternal sin" (Mark 3:29). To this proof text he added 1 John 5:16: "If anyone sees his brother committing a sin not leading to death, he shall ask and God will for him give life to those who commit sin not leading to death. There is a sin leading to death; I do not say he should make request for this."

The disturbed young man had integrated these two difficult Scriptures into his sick emotional system. Finally it became evident that he did not really want to be forgiven. Instead he clung tenaciously to his guilt—the way a small child clutches a familiar doll or a tattered "security" blanket.

Plumbing the depths of this man's warped emotions required more skill and time than this pastor possessed. But I concluded that the depth of his sin—and perhaps this is what made it unforgivable—was his failure to believe that God could have forgiven him. Indeed, that God *wanted* to forgive, cleanse, and to provide for him a new and better life in Christ.

Perhaps when one says, *"God cannot,"* that becomes the unforgivable sin. Blasphemy against one member of the Holy Trinity is blasphemy against all three.

Jesus said, "With God *all things* are possible" (Matt. 19:26). Limiting God is the very heart of unbelief, for this denies every other profession of faith about Him and also denies the biblical record of His power over all that He has made (and that includes us).

Forgiveness

The unhappy, emotionally disturbed young man represented an attitude that is all too common: reluctance to accept the forgiveness which God has clearly promised in the Bible and which Christ died on Calvary to provide (1 John 2:2).

When God's forgiveness is accepted, "salvation is no longer some remote idea of perfection, forever inaccessible. It is a Person, Jesus Christ, who comes to us, comes to be with us, in our homes and in our hearts. Remorse is silenced by His absolution. He substitutes for it one other single question, the one He put to the Apostle Peter: "Do you love Me?" (John 21:15). We must answer that question, and find in our personal attachment to Jesus Christ peace for our souls." [2]

When someone has believed in Christ but still has trouble feeling free from guilt, that person probably has only a mind relationship with Christ, one which remains on the intellectual level and has not yet penetrated into the levels of feeling and emotion where guilt lurks and breeds.

A world-famous missionary evangelist and author used to say that we are saved when Jesus becomes

---

[2] Tournier, *Guilt and Grace*, p. 187.

Lord of our *minds;* later we are sanctified when Jesus becomes Lord of the *inner-self,* the realm of feelings and emotions and motivations.

The problem is this: How can your faith be deepened to include *all* of you? How can the whole person, intellect *and* emotions, be brought under the Lordship of Jesus Christ?

Until this happens, your guilt problem will not be really solved. You will be like the old man who was hiking down a country road carrying a heavy sack of potatoes to market.

A neighbor, also heading to market in a wagon, stopped beside the old man. "Ride with me," he invited. "There's no need for you to carry that heavy load all the way to town."

The old man accepted gladly. He climbed into the wagon and together the two men proceeded toward town. But the driver noticed that the old man was still clutching the heavy sack of potatoes, bowing low under its weight.

"There's no need for you to keep on carrying that heavy load," he said. "Why don't you set it down on the floor of the wagon?"

"No," the old man replied, "I don't want to make it harder for the horse."

Incomplete Faith

The old man was no more foolish than the person who knows that Christ has atoned for his sins on the cross, but who, nevertheless, keeps listening to those words, "GUILTY! GUILTY! GUILTY!"

Why does this happen so often? Why do so many fail to accept God's forgiveness?

Many people think of guilt and forgiveness only in spiritual terms, divorced from the nitty-gritty of daily life. Christ's death on the cross for me is something that happened long ago on a hill far away. I receive this gift by faith and that is the end of the transaction. It is all grace—there is nothing I need to do except receive and utilize the gift of divine forgiveness which Christ has made available by His death upon the cross. I believe. I accept the gift. Period.

Many people never get beyond the partial truth. They fail to get hold of the larger truth—genuine repentance involves giving as well as receiving.

It is true, of course, that Christ has made the sacrifice to completely atone for your sin. As a result, the gift of forgiveness is offered to you, free for the taking.

To stop at this point, however, is to go only halfway. Faith which genuinely apprehends and appropriates the atoning death of Christ instinctively responds first to Christ Himself and then to others. There should be no such thing as "just me and Jesus" unrelated to daily life. This is not faith; it is heresy if one's faith stops with accepting Christ's gift and ignores human relationships. James described this as "faith, if it has no works, is dead, being by itself" (James 2:17). Such was the supposed but tragically incomplete faith of some people Jesus described in His dissertation on the Last Judgment (Matt. 25:31-46).

"When the Son of Man comes in His glory, and all the angels with Him, then He will sit on His glorious throne. And all the nations [people] will be gathered before Him; and He will separate them one from another, as the shepherd separates the sheep from the goats" (vv. 31-32).

Many who did not expect to enter God's eternal kingdom will be surprised when He says to them, "Come, you who are blessed of My Father, inherit the kingdom prepared for you from the foundation of the world" (v. 34).

But many who are confident of their good standing with God will be shocked when they hear the King say to them, "Depart from Me, accursed ones, into the eternal fire which has been prepared for the devil and his angels" (v. 41).

Why will some go into the everlasting fires of hell while others enter the never-ending glory of the Father's eternal kingdom? Those saved from the fires had reached out both to God and their neighbors. Their faith involved not only the "spiritual," but also involved the nitty-gritty dimension of providing clothes, food, and companionship for people in need. Such is the faith proved genuine by works of love, inspired by the source of all love, God Himself.

The damned—many of them religious people—will be shocked on Judgment Day. Somehow they had failed to realize that authentic, saving faith has a "people" dimension. Apparently their faith was only a spiritual "God and me." It was finally condemned as inadequate.

Both the Old and New Testaments clearly teach that authentic faith must include God *and* neighbors. Isaiah said it bluntly, condemning the spiritual-only religion of ancient Jerusalem: "So when you spread out your hands in prayer, I will hide my eyes from you. Yes, even though you multiply prayers, I will not listen. Your hands are full of bloodshed" (Isa. 1:15).

How does this apply to finding forgiveness?

Those who accept only God's gift of forgiveness have an incomplete repentance. They are like a lamp which has all the capacity to give light but remains dark. It cannot burn until the lamp is plugged into a source of power. Till this happens, the lamp may be beautiful and perfect—but it is useless.

The faith of a Christian may be theologically perfect, but it may never produce light, warmth, and illumination. It is not authentic faith; it doesn't relate to the daily life of that Christian.

Deeds Appropriate to Repentance

Speaking to King Agrippa, the Apostle Paul said that he had been telling people "that they should repent and turn to God, performing deeds appropriate to repentance" (Acts 26:20). The absence of "deeds appropriate to repentance" is what keeps God's forgiveness like an open circuit. Deeds of repentance are needed to close the circuit, allowing God's forgiving power to flow, cleansing and healing. It is not a matter of doing all that God requires. Paul said, "For we are [God's] workmanship, created in Christ Jesus for good works" (Eph. 2:10).

We mentioned earlier a minister who refused to call a seminary professor and confess a sin of long ago. A phone call or a letter would have been a deed "appropriate to repentance." Without this, the minister's intellectual acceptance of pardon obtained through the Cross did not bring victory over his guilt feelings. His repentance was only partial; no peace from God flowed through the open circuit between him and God.

A similar incident had a happy ending. A news service reported this story about a minister in Chattanooga, Tenn.:

> He confessed that he stole $3,000 from a food store 14 years ago "while obsessed with gambling and wild ways" and has begun restitution of the money.
>
> "Unbelievable," said Don Blevins, store manager, when the pastor of the World's Church of the Living God arrived at the store with $50 as the first payment.
>
> "Now I can feel truly free," the minister said. "I can look my people in the eyes and tell them that I have sinned, but I have sought and received forgiveness from God and man."
>
> Police say the minister will remain free because the statute of limitations has long since run out on the crime.[3]

Imagine the electric impact on the store owner! On the employees. On members of the church, the whole community.

"Here," they say with awe, "is a religion with *power!* This man is not just playing church, he is living a changed life."

Thus deeds or works "appropriate to repentance" become a powerful instrument for Christian witness. Many people will listen with respect to a

---

[3] Evangelical Press News Service, dated Aug. 9, 1975.

man who represents a God who instills in His followers such honesty and courage.

Some people might say he is crazy. But more (perhaps even some of those who mock) will inwardly envy his idealism, his courage, and his integrity.

Another recent example of deeds "appropriate to repentance" comes out of Watergate: the dramatic admission of Chuck Colson, ex-presidential aide, who confessed wrongdoing to the judge and thus set himself up for a jail sentence.

What happened?

Colson, President Nixon's "tough guy" or "hatchet man," became a Christian—right in the middle of the Watergate turmoil. His "deeds appropriate to repentance" were reported in a nationally syndicated article:

> The surprise guilty plea by Charles W. Colson to a charge of obstruction of justice this week came after two prayer meetings with Capitol Hill colleagues . . .
>
> A week or 10 days ago, Colson went to Sen. Harold Hughes and the other three members of their Monday morning prayer group with this thought of pleading guilty.
>
> "We prayed with him, we counseled him, we assured him we felt it was the right thing to do," Hughes said . . . "He felt a moral obligation to right these wrongs and to help the country in these difficult times . . ."
>
> The [prayer] meeting lasted until 1:00 A.M. Eight and one-half hours later, Colson, ramrod straight as the Marine officer he once was, and his wife dabbing at her eyes, were in . . . the courtroom . . .
>
> There was never any doubt in Hughes' mind that

Colson would come through. "I knew he would," Hughes said. "A man can't have a complete commitment without eventually arriving at the conclusion that he must straighten out his life." [4]

The principle is clear: "Deeds appropriate to repentance" complete the circuit of forgiveness. And through that closed connection, God heals the wounds of guilt. A lack of such "deeds" is one reason why so many people are never able to really feel clean, feel fully forgiven, even though they believe "correctly" about Christ's atoning death on the cross.

Incomplete Forgiveness

A strange and frightening fact is that some do not find God's forgiveness because their hearts are hardened. Events which drive some people toward God in repentance seem to drive the hardened of heart farther from God.

The student of history will recall how in past centuries, when wars, famines, and pestilence have decimated whole nations, the survivors in most cases have become worse rather than better. One thinks of the days of the plague in Paris in the 17th and 18th centuries, when terror seized the populace. Yet there was a turning from, instead of turning to, God, and the frenzied citizens plunged into all kinds of vile excesses and orgies of infamy in order to help forget the ever-present danger.[5]

Another reason for failure to experience forgive-

---

[4] Wesley G. Pippert, United Press International, June 5, 1974.
[5] Ironside, *Except Ye Repent*, p. 108.

ness is failure to take God at His word concerning His *desire* and His *ability* to cleanse the sinner entirely.

A key scripture is 1 John 1:9: "If we confess our sins, He is faithful and righteous to forgive us our sins and to cleanse us from all unrighteousness." The word *all* is the key; it is a promise of total cleansing. Nothing, apparently, lies beyond the sovereign God's ability to wipe away our uncleanness.

God *has* this ability. Do you believe it?

In the Bible *believe* means much more than saying yes to certain facts such as "one plus one equals two," or "the earth revolves around the sun."

Believe, in the Bible, means "trusting, putting your whole weight upon, as a person rests in a chair." To *believe* means to live your life on the basis of what you know to be true. Thus, in the Bible, *believe* always requires action, some demonstration that you trust God and will do as He says.

Consider again the confession of the minister in Chattanooga. Some godless people think him crazy for admitting a sin when he hadn't been caught. But belief, for this minister, meant acting according to what he knows to be true. Failure to act would constitute unbelief. Thus we circle back to the fundamental teaching that "faith [belief], if it has no works, is dead, being by itself" (James 2:17).

If you truly believe that God has forgiven you, then you are compelled to live accordingly. Otherwise you have not yet actually believed. You are only pretending and this will prevent you from fully accepting God's forgiveness.

Does God really *want* to forgive me? *Is* forgiveness His desire? Can I count on this?

God spoke to ancient Israel, and speaks today to believers in every generation, saying, "Come now, and let us reason together . . . Though your sins are as scarlet they will be white as snow; though they are red like crimson, they will be like wool" (Isa. 1:18).

Here is another promise of total cleansing, spoken by the same God who said to His people, "You shall be holy [pure, blameless, unblemished], for I the Lord your God am holy" (Lev. 19:2).

When we really want to know what God is like, we look at Jesus Christ. From the final hours of His earthly life we receive the greatest assurance that our heavenly Father is a forgiving God.

Jesus had just been nailed to the cross by Roman soldiers. They waited around, watching to see that His execution was carried out as decreed. It would have been human for Jesus to curse them. But instead, He revealed the pardoning heart of God when He spoke from the cross: "Father, forgive them; for they do not know what they are doing" (Luke 23:34).

These sublime words prove that God desires to pardon the worst sinners—even those who tortured and killed His only Son. Today He still wants to pardon those who are rejecting His Son.

7

A Young Man Forgiven

The year was 740 B.C.[1]

The place: Jerusalem.

The nation faced a crisis perhaps as frightening to the ancient Jews as Watergate was to many Americans. King Uzziah had just died and his reign of 52 years, one of the longest in Judah's history, had been a source of security. Uzziah provided a much-needed time of continuity, contrasting sharply with previous kings who had ruled briefly and died violently.[2]

The nation prospered under King Uzziah, but the final years of his reign had been marked by

---

[1] Francis Davidson, ed., *The New Bible Commentary* (Grand Rapids: Eerdmans Publishing Company, 1953), p. 556.

[2] J. D. Douglas, ed., *The New Bible Dictionary* (Grand Rapids: Eerdmans Publishing Company, 1962), p. 1307.

the king's affliction with leprosy and his withdrawal from public life. Still, Uzziah had been an effective king (2 Chron. 26).

His death brought the nation to a critical point. Who would be their new king? Would he lead them wisely? Would he obey God and lead the people of Judah into continued prosperity? Or would he, like some past kings, turn away from the Holy One of Israel and thus bring disaster?

Isaiah's Experience

A young man in Jerusalem, Isaiah, whose name means "Jehovah saves" or "Jehovah is salvation," emerged as a prophet. "In the year of King Uzziah's death" (Isa. 6:1) he visited the great Jerusalem temple. Perhaps he came to pray for his country. Perhaps he came because, in time of trouble, he wanted to be closer to God in the awesome place where God's glory mysteriously centered.

In the temple, God made Himself known to young Isaiah. Today we might call it a "mountain-top experience." It changed his life. It fixed his feet upon a difficult path that would make him one of the most controversial people of his nation— hated, feared, and usually misunderstood as the Lord's prophet. Young Isaiah was to be used by God in remarkable ways, and through him God would speak to ancient Judah, and the Book of Isaiah, preserved in the Scriptures, would speak to God's people for all generations.

It all began when a young man visited the temple in time of national crisis. There occurred a dynamic

experience of worship which includes all that we
have been talking about in the preceding chapters:
guilt, repentance, divine cleansing, and "deeds appropriate to repentance."

Who knows what we might achieve if we faced
our guilt as Isaiah did. So let's look carefully at his
life-transforming experience.

The Place of God's Presence

"In the year of King Uzziah's death, I saw the
Lord" (6:1), the young prophet wrote. Here is the
place where guilt must be dealt with: in the presence of the Lord. In Isaiah's case, it happened in
the temple, the "holy place" of his nation.

Today, there is nothing like the great Jerusalem
temple where Isaiah was confronted by the living
God. Since the death and resurrection of Christ
and the coming of the Holy Spirit, God's glory is
no longer concentrated in one location, but "where
two or three have gathered together in My name,
there I am in their midst" (Matt. 18:20). This is
the mark of the true Church: where people gather
in the name of Christ. He is with them, and Christ's
dwelling in ordinary people is great glory to God.

Many people have strange ideas about the church.
Some think it is a place where only "good" people
congregate.

I recall one difficult marriage counseling situation. When I became involved as the couple's pastor, the husband and wife had drifted so far apart
they were headed toward the divorce court. One
Sunday morning, the husband, who worshiped only
occasionally, heard the Gospel and accepted Christ

as his Saviour. He started studying the Bible and became active in a church prayer and study group. It was exciting to see God working in his life.

Then I began getting acquainted with the wife —a distant and nominal church member. She was angry with her husband for many reasons, but most of all she resented his new activity in the church.

One afternoon she exploded. "He's such a big hypocrite! He goes to church all the time, acting like a goodie-goodie. You should see how he is at home!"

To the wife, church was a place for people who had no serious needs or problems. People who attended church were "hypocrites" if they had hangups and imperfections. On the other hand, many congregations are offended when people with obvious sin problems show up in church.

Other people are suspect if they are markedly "different," sport beards, or wear unconventional clothes. Such people often get a cold shoulder because they challenge the image of a church for "good people"—people just like us.

I was once involved in counseling a disturbed young man, a victim of drugs, alcohol, job failure, and divorce. I worked for two months to become this drifter's friend, to listen, to await the right moment to introduce him to Christ. Most of our visits were late at night in the empty church; I accommodated myself to the unconventional schedule of this man.

Progress was being made. The troubled young man had at last found a friend and had begun to consider the church as a place of caring, a place where he might be helped. One evening he showed up early. He sat in the sanctuary awaiting our time together.

The church janitor, a retired policeman, was upset when he saw this stranger with ragged clothes, stringy long hair, peculiar smell, and off-another-planet attitude. These differences aroused the ex-policeman's hostility. Pulling his badge (which he always carried), he ordered the young man to get out of the church and never to come back. He never did.

The church, someone has wisely said, is not a roosting place for saints but a hospital for sinners. It is a place for people to come when, aching, frightened, and weary of life, they yearn for God's healing, cleansing touch upon their lives. The church that forgets its role as a center for redemption of sinners is like a hospital that does not minister to the physical problems of patients, or a watch repairman who doesn't fix watches.

A Too-Small God

Isaiah did not come to the Jerusalem temple for human counseling nor fellowship with the saints. He came to meet the Lord and he saw "the Lord sitting on a throne, lofty and exalted, with the train of His robe filling the temple. Seraphim [angels] stood above Him, each having six wings; with two he covered his face, and with two he covered his feet, and with two he flew. And one called out to another and said, 'Holy, Holy, Holy, is the Lord of hosts, the whole world is full of His glory.' And the foundations of the thresholds trembled at the voice of Him who called out, while the temple was filled with smoke" (6:1-4).

Who can fully explain or understand what Isaiah here described? There is really no point in probing the mysteries of *how* God showed Himself to Isaiah. The point for our consideration is that God revealed Himself in personal experience as majestic, holy, high above us.

Today people consciously or unconsciously try to reduce the gulf between a holy God and sinners. God has been reduced to the status of chum, buddy or helper who "has no hands but our hands." He has become small and inadequate. Such a manufactured deity has no actual power. He cannot deal, as Lord, with our sins and our guilts. He cannot cleanse and heal, for he is not the God of the Bible. Instead, this is a false god, an idol to be subservient to us.

This is why so many people today find no relief for their guilt: Their god is too small. Only the living God, He who made full atonement for all our sins, can cleanse us from the guilt they produce within us.

Is your God too small? That may be your greatest spiritual problem—the reason that your spiritual life has outward form, but lacks real power and joy. If you try to domesticate God so he won't disturb your life, don't expect that He is going to significantly change or help you.

When God Confronts

Encountered in the temple of Jerusalem by the Holy One of Israel, Isaiah responded with an admission of his sin: "I said, 'Woe is me, for I am ruined! Because I am a man of unclean lips, and I live among a people of unclean lips, and I have seen the King, the Lord of hosts'" (6:5).

In the presence of God, we must admit our littleness, our pettiness, our ugliness, and the context of sin in which we live. The radical contrast between our finiteness and the majesty of God leads to real confession—true repentance. But if your highest standard of comparison is other people, or your God is small (minimized so as to be undisturbing), then you will remain complacent. You can escape the humbling confrontation with the Holy One.

Isaiah seems to have some connection with the royal family of king Uzziah, so he was probably among the social "upper crust." [3] If all this made young Isaiah complacent about himself as he entered the Temple to pray, any self-satisfaction was exposed in the blinding light of God's holiness. Instead of feeling smug, the young man was humbled, crushed. Perhaps for the first time, he became aware of his own uncleanness and the uncleanness of his society.

The church which fails to teach the holiness of God is not likely to be the place where God convicts of sin. And where there is no such conviction, there will be no redemption, for redemption requires that we humble ourselves and trust only in Christ.

Many churches today preach ethics, psychology,

---

[3] Davidson, *The New Bible Commentary*, p. 556.

or salvation through relationships between people. Some preach rules for holy living. Others preach the importance of speaking in tongues, healing, or confronting the injustices in the world. Some churces which seem more orthodox preach Jesus as Friend and dwell continually on the experience of first coming to know Him. Others talk about a God of Creation—or talk about the "Christian walk" as if what we *do* as followers of Christ is most important.

Missing from such churches, whether liberal or conservative, is the High God whom Isaiah met— the mysterious and terrible God whose face cannot be seen by mortal men. He is the Holy One whom the psalmist described in these terms: "The Lord is high above all nations; His glory is above the heavens" (Ps. 113:4). Isaiah later wrote of this God: "For as the heavens are higher than the earth, so are My ways higher than your ways, and My thoughts than your thoughts" (Isa. 55:9).

Isaiah's Guilt Cauterized

Young Isaiah's guilt was removed by the same holy God who first roused that guilt: "Then one of the seraphim flew to me, with a burning coal in his hand which he had taken from the altar with tongs. And he touched my mouth with it and said, 'Behold, this has touched your lips; and your iniquity is taken away, and your sin is forgiven'" (vv. 6-7).

God Himself acted to help Isaiah. The lips which had confessed the young man's uncleanness were touched with holy fire. This burned away uncleanness as a red hot probe cauterizes a wound to prevent infection and begin the process of healing.

John the Baptist came preaching just before Jesus was revealed as the Christ. As the last in a long line of prophets, John said, "As for me, I baptize you in water for repentance; but He who is coming after me [Christ] is mightier than I, and I am not even fit to remove His sandals; He Himself will baptize you with the Holy Spirit and with fire" (Matt. 3:11).

Touching and cleansing sinful lives, as a burning fire of holiness, is the special ministry of Jesus. And so Isaiah's experience in the temple was a preview of a fire-cleansing that is now available and happens to all who turn to Christ. When genuine repentance occurs, God's cauterizing touch "makes the wounded whole."

The Chattanooga minister who courageously confessed that he had stolen must have experienced God's fire-cleansing. Nothing less than this could cause a man to be so bold in repentance; psychology or mere self-realization could not have produced so remarkable a result.

Are you unable to get rid of nagging guilt, even though you believe that Christ paid for your sin with His life? Then seek the touch of fire from the living God. Ask Him to cauterize you. Ask for the assurance given to young Isaiah: "Your iniquity is taken away, and your sin is forgiven." This is God's will for each redeemed child. "Now may the God of peace Himself sanctify you entirely; and may your spirit and soul and body be preserved complete, without blame at the coming of our Lord Jesus Christ. Faithful is He who calls you, and He also will bring it to pass" (1 Thes. 5:23-24).

The Call to Service

"Then I heard the voice of the Lord, saying, 'Whom shall I send, and who will go for us?'" (Isa. 6:8) God's call to service always follows His forgiveness. He cleanses us, as a surgeon sterilizes his instruments, in order to use us.

Isaiah heard God's summons. When we are cleansed of guilt, we are able to hear God or openly admit that we have heard Him. A familiar "game" people play with God is not admitting they have heard His voice. Pretending to be deaf, they ignore Him and "do their own thing" like Jonah, who attempted to escape the will of the Lord by running in the opposite direction.

Real cleansing does away with such pretending. Isaiah answered God directly: "Here I am. Send me!"

Isaiah volunteered without asking God for details. In this Isaiah was like Abraham, who heard God's voice and "when he was called, obeyed by going out to a place which he was to receive for an inheritance; and he went out, not knowing where he was going" (Heb. 11:8).

A passage in Tennyson's *The Charge of the Light Brigade* applies to the unquestioning obedience of those purified in heart: "Theirs not to reason why, theirs but to do and die." When men blindly obey a military command, it has the mark of fanaticism. But when it is a matter of unquestioning obedience to the Holy One, the Bible calls it faith (Hebrews 11).

Until we, like Isaiah, obey God without questions, we can expect to doubt our salvation, to continue to play "games" with God, and to quibble about doing what God wants us to do or going where He wants us to go.

Isaiah's Mandate

God had called Isaiah to complete a difficult mission. God would send him as divine messenger to a people so blind and hardened of heart that they would persist in sin to their destruction. God explained the tough job ahead: "Go tell this people: keep on listening, but do not perceive; keep on looking, but do not understand. Render the hearts of this people insensitive, and their eyes dim, lest they see with their eyes, hear with their ears, understand with their hearts, and repent and be healed" (6:9-10).

The doom of Isaiah's people had already been sealed. Generations of disobedience had fixed them in a pattern of chronic sin. God, who sees the future as well as the past, knew Judah was destined for destruction. Isaiah's job was not to save them, but to hold before them their sin and make plain that the impending disaster was the consequence of ignoring the Holy One. Long ago He had promised to be their God, with the condition that they be His obedient people.

Jesus' mission was to die upon a cross. Isaiah's mission was to announce that the Holy One would eventually pour out His wrath upon all uncleanness. God has work for you to do. He does not always call us to be "successful"—as we Americans use that word. All does not end in happiness for Christians; we live in a fallen world where wrong often triumphs over right.

It is not your business to question God. "Who are you, O man, who answers back to God? The thing molded will not say to the molder, 'Why did you make me like this,' will it? Or does not the potter have a right over the clay, to make from the same lump one vessel for honorable use, and another for common use?" (Rom. 9:20-21). "Why do you complain against Him, that he does not give an account of all His doings?" (Job 33:13)

Isaiah, learning the difficulty of his service for God, did not ask for a new and easier assignment. He only asked, "Lord, how long?" (Isa. 6:11).

God, who is utterly honest, told Isaiah that his mission would continue until the nation's disobedience had ben punished by the final destruction of the kingdom of Judah and the city of Jerusalem: "Until cities are devastated and without inhabitant, houses are without people, and the land is desolate, the Lord has removed men far away, and the forsaken places are many in the midst of the land. Yet there will be a tenth portion in it, and it will again be subject to burning, like a terebinth or an oak whose stump remains when it is felled. The holy seed is its stump" (6:11-13).

Interpreting this prophesy is beyond the scope of this book. But in Isaiah we have seen some basic principles of guilt, forgiveness, and cleansing.

They apply to your life as much as to the life of a young man who was forgiven by God some 2,600 years ago.

1) f —
2) < —
3) s —

8

The Prince
of Forgiveness

As an architect looks at blueprints to learn how a house should be built, the true Christian looks to Jesus Christ for direction (and correction) in understanding the Christian faith and in living the Christian life. The Apostle Paul was inspired by the Holy Spirit to write: "God, who said, 'Light shall shine out of darkness,' is the One who has shone in our hearts to give the light of the knowledge of the glory of God in the face of Christ" (2 Cor. 4:6). "[You] have put on the new self who is being renewed to a true knowledge according to the image of the One who created him, a renewal in which there is no distinction between Greek and Jew, circumcised and uncircumcised, barbarian, Scythian, slave and freeman, but Christ is all, and in all" (Col. 3:11-12).

For centuries, hymnists and poets have tried to

express the central importance of Jesus in word and music. Charles Carroll Albertson said:

He is the Ancient Wisdom of the World
The Word Creative, Beautiful and True,
The Nameless of innumerable names,
Ageless forever, yet forever New.[1]

"In Christ is all the God we know" wrote the poet Edwin Markham.[2]

Being A Christian

In a time when "being a Christian" means many different things, it needs to be emphasized that the heart of being a Christian is becoming like our Saviour. The Apostle Paul wrote, "From the very beginning God decided that those who came to Him—and all along He knew who would—should become like His Son, so that His Son would be the First, with many brothers" (Rom. 8:29, LB).

It is essential, therefore, that we look at Christ's dealing with guilt. We need to see how He extended forgiveness, making a wonderful reality of the ancient promise: "As far as the east is from the west, so far has He removed our transgressions from us" (Ps. 103:12).

A Woman Of Samaria

One day Jesus met a woman at the well of Sychar, a city in Samaria. (See John 4:1-42.) Here was an unclean woman, a moral outcast. Perhaps this was

---

[1] James Dalton Morrison, ed., *Masterpieces of Religious Verse* (New York: Harper and Brothers, Publishers, 1948), p. 137.

[2] Morrison, *Masterpieces of Religious Verse,* p. 140.

why she was at the well alone—the other women of the community shunned her. A woman who had five husbands and was now living with a sixth man would be considered something of a swinger even in our sexually permissive society. But in ancient times, her conduct was scandalous—particularly in a small town where everybody would know of her escapades.

The Verbal Cloud

This woman carried not only a heavy load of water but an even heavier burden of guilt. Her response to Jesus suggests that she had developed an ability to protect herself with a glib tongue; she showed great verbal skill in her conversation with Jesus.

This is one of the games some guilty people play —they throw up a screen of words to draw attention away from their sins and weaknesses. Such people are like an octopus, which, when attacked or frightened, squirts out a cloud of ink. The ink turns the water black, and in the confusion, the octopus scuttles away to hide from its enemy.

The woman at the well first tried to hide behind the hostility existing between Jews and Samaritans (John 4:9).

Jesus refused to play her game. He didn't launch into a discussion of the tension between Jews and Samaritans. He didn't scorn the Samaritans, as religious Jews usually did. Nor did He immediately accuse the woman of sin. Being God, He knew all about her sin, but He wisely waited till a "right" time. Our Lord did not charge in, like a bull in a china shop, and preach at the woman. Instead, He gently and easily focused her attention on Himself.

Here is an important lesson about dealing with guilty people. Their first need is not a scolding. (Most are already painfully aware that they have done wrong.) Rather, let Jesus Christ become the center of consideration. He alone has power to cleanse. Only He can save the guilty person from sin's effects.

On a long automobile trip recently, we heard one radio preacher after another thundering against sin in general and sinners in particular. Apparently they expected their verbal barrages (complete with shouts, speaking in tongues, and pounding the pulpit) to somehow bring guilty listeners to repentance. Rarely was Christ mentioned by these radio preachers—except as a magic formula. His name was plugged in at the end, or used as an occasional catchword.

If Jesus had approached the woman at the well in this way, she may never have faced honestly the ugliness of her life.

Practical Matters

The woman's next attempt at diversion was an obvious problem: Jesus did not have a container with which to draw water from the well (4:11). How often people seek to divert attention from their guilt by preoccupation with practical matters. How will I pay all the bills? But, Lord, first I have to take care of my farm or bury my father. Countless "practical" matters may provide an escape from honest encounters with truth—about God, about ourselves, about others.

A woman is constantly ill. She goes from one doctor to another, spending thousands of dollars on examinations, medicine, and treatments. Her fragile health is a constant subject of conversation. It provides a convenient escape from facing the need to repent of long-buried sin, the need to present her life to God.

Tradition

The woman did not succeed in diverting Jesus' attention to His lack of a water pot, so she brought up another subject: tradition. She said, "You are not greater than our father Jacob, are You, who gave us the well, and drank of it himself, and his sons and cattle?" (4:12) What a skillful way to goad a religious Jew into argument—Jews despised the Samaritans, who were a mixture of Jewish and pagan blood and tradition.

But with skill and loving patience the Master parried this diversion also. He kept pressing her real need: living or spiritual water which alone would assuage the thirst of her guilt. It alone would bring cleanness and peace to a woman who had lived with so many husbands.

Again we see the basic principle: Keep the focus on Jesus, His Person, His power, His promises, His ability to make the wounded whole. He Himself said, "And I, *if I be lifted up* from the earth, will draw all men to Myself" (John 12:32).

If you really want to help people, you must never forget that the ultimate Helper is Christ.

He is the Only way by which people can find God
(John 14:6).

The Deepest Need

Jesus touched the woman's deepest need when He
offered eternal life and an end to thirst (4:13-14).
The desire for these lay beneath her guilt and constitutes the basic human yearning which Augustine
described in a beautiful prayer, "Thou hast made
us for Thyself, O God, and we are restless until
we find our rest in Thee." Our Lord promised,
"Blessed are those who hunger and thirst for righteousness, for they shall be satisfied" (Matt. 5:6).

Jesus touched the woman's spiritual antecham-
ber and blocked her attempts at diversion. So her
conversation shifted from escape to receptiveness:
"Sir, give me this water." (4:15).

Of course, she was only beginning to understand. She still thought of thirst and water in
terms of what could be drawn from the well of
Jacob (4:15).

Finally, only after her guilt-defenses had been
breached three times, Jesus moved directly upon
her guilt. He said, "Go, call your husband, and
come here" (4:16).

Jesus did not berate her; He did not call her
a loose woman, a whore, or an adulteress. Instead,
He made one devastating request. It showed her
there was no use pretending, no use hiding the
truth about herself. Jesus' request also let her
know that He did not scorn her for her sin. The
Holy confronted the unholy without bitterness,
without accusations or superiority.

Timely Words

Often kindly spoken words can accomplish more than a thousand diatribes and denunciations. Perhaps our greatest need, in dealing with the guilty, is to say the right things and ask the right questions at the right times. French atheist Voltaire hit upon a profound truth when he said, "Judge a man by his questions rather than by his answers." Fortunately, the Holy Spirit can give us the questions. He can direct not only in the phrasing but in the very tone of concern and honest compassion.

Damage can easily be done when we let our feelings and personal "hangups" direct our dealings with one carrying a burden of guilt.

My own greatest failures in trying to help people have come when "I" took over. But those times when "I" was guided by the Holy Spirit, God has spoken through me to the guilty.

Please notice that Jesus did not avoid the unpleasant subject of her sin. At the proper moment He confronted her with astonishing directness: "You have said well, 'I have no husband', for you have had five husbands; and the one whom you now have is not your husband" (John 4:17-18).

This contrasts sharply with so many unrealistic attempts to be "Christian" by avoiding any mention of sin. Psychiatrist Karl Menninger expressed this phenomenon by giving his 1973 book the revealing title, *What Ever Became of Sin?* Liberals have largely removed sin from their vocabulary as sin relates to personal behavior. They may apply the term to certain individual and social evils such as racism and sexism but seldom to such individual sins as homosexuality, drunkenness, sexual promiscuity, and abortion as the murder of unborn infants.

At the proper time Jesus faced directly the fact of personal sin. Read again the account of our Lord and the woman at the well. There was not a trace of self-righteousness when Jesus pointed out her transgressions. He did this indirectly, but with devastating effect, by stating one fact—the fact of her marital history.

Her response was surprising. "She said to Him, 'Sir, I perceive that you are a prophet'" (4:19). An oblique admission—but then she quickly turned away from this painful subject and steered the conversation to a less personal topic: religious tradition. "Our fathers worshiped in this mountain; and you people say that Jerusalem is the place where men ought to worship" (v. 20).

Jesus did not drag the conversation back to the woman's sin and guilt. Instead, He was content to follow her lead and speak about true worship (vv. 21-24). What a strange place to talk about this. But is it? Our Lord suggests that worship of the heavenly Father "in spirit and truth" is the ultimate answer to human guilt.

True Worship

We seldom relate worship to the removal of guilt. Well-meaning counselors may prescribe "going to church," but real worship is all too rare—even among those professing an evangelical faith.

One Sunday during a vacation we stopped to

worship in a church whose denomination boasts proudly of its orthodoxy. Seeking an experience of worship, we were saddened by a succession of announcements, an attendance contest, and a sermon in which the speaker (it was not preaching) mumbled some personal anecdotes and then warned everyone they would burn in hell unless they accepted Christ as their Saviour. The meeting ended with the listless singing of "Just as I Am." The congregation obviously was going through a tedious ritual. Lukewarm was the kindest description of this "service."

Worship? Not if worship means praising God with power, joy, and genuineness. Not if worship is directed by the Holy Spirit (He is never dull) and "truth" means holding forth the eternal realities of God.

Unfortunately, much that passes for worship is not "in spirit and in truth." Instead, it is the remnant of tent-meeting evangelism, without the freshness and fire. Such "worship" is simply embalmed ritual; it does not cure the sin-sick soul, nor does it confront the sinner and the backslider with God's awesome holiness and majesty.

Is our worship so genuine that guilt will be removed by the God of wholeness? If a church fails to worship in "spirit" and in "truth" is it actually the Church of Jesus Christ?

The End of Guilt

Jesus' conversation with the woman at the well came to a climax when Jesus revealed Himself as the Christ (4:26). Here is where all discussion about guilt must end: in the acknowledged presence of the only begotten Son of God, He who made perfect atonement for all sin.

The woman's response was to go hurrying back to her village, where she called out an invitation: "Come, see a man who told me all the things I have done; this is not the Christ, is it?" (v. 29). Thus she admitted her sordid past before the whole community. Perhaps people came to Jesus expecting an X-rated revelation of the woman's lurid life. This familiar story of Jesus and the woman at the well contains many valuable insights into guilt and the guilty. It seems evident that the way we deal with guilt often differs from the ways of Jesus. The measure of this departure helps to explain why the church today has only begun to realize Jesus' remarkable promise, "Truly, truly, I say to you, he who believes in Me, the works that I do shall he do also; and greater works than these shall he do; because I go to the Father" (John 14:12).

The Gospel of John reports another encounter between Jesus and a sinful woman (8:1-11). The woman caught committing adultery had something in common with the woman whom Jesus met at the well of Sychar. The absence of condemnation by Jesus is perhaps the outstanding characteristic of both incidents. The words Jesus spoke to the second sinner were almost clinical: "Neither do I condemn you; go your way; from now on sin no more" (v. 11).

Her response is not recorded. We have no way of knowing whether she took Jesus' advice or whether she slipped back into adultery.

In this incident Jesus' handling of the crowd is particularly noteworthy. Jewish Law gave the men perfect right to stone to death one guilty of adultery. The Law makes clear however, that guilt may involve both parties (Lev. 20:10).

Each man in the crowd perhaps carried a stone to throw at the humiliated woman. Likely some also carried a load of suppressed guilt over their own sex sins. Some had perhaps committed secret adultery. But the real cause of universal guilt was exposed in these words of Jesus: "You have heard that it was said, 'You shall not commit adultery'; but I say to you that every one who looks on a woman to lust for her has committed adultery with her already in his heart" (Matt. 5:27-28).

When He spoke to the crowd preparing to stone the adulteress in John 8, Jesus knew that each man harbored guilt for his own lust. That is why Jesus said to them, "He who is without sin among you, let him be the first to throw a stone at her" (v. 7).

Jesus convicted them with a challenge that penetrated their hypocrisy like a spear. Like an X ray it revealed their "game" of guilt projection, transferring to the woman their own guilt.

We need to recognize the commonness of guilt projection. Often people want to transfer to others their own guilt. Usually this is an unconscious effort—that is hard to recognize. It just happens as a result of our sinful human nature.

Jesus Christ always recognizes the games you are playing. In love and heavenly wisdom He ministers to you when you need to be made aware of your own true guilt. Jesus does this. And when you need assurance that your guilt has been taken away, Jesus supplies this also. Whatever you need, Jesus meets it completely. He is the One who "heals all your diseases" (Ps. 103:3)—the greatest of which may be guilt.

9

The Laboratory
of Forgiveness

It was one of those classic church fights. For a
long time the women of the small Midwestern
congregation had complained about the grubby,
ugly women's washroom in the church basement.
But, in spite of the grumbling, nobody did anything.

Then one year the youth group became unusu-
ally active. After church one day the youth leader
and several teenagers approached the pastor.

"We would like to do something for the church,"
their spokesman said. "The ladies' room is pretty
run-down. We thought maybe we could paint it.
Would that be all right?"

Astonished that anyone would volunteer, the
pastor stammered, "Why, yes . . . that would be
wonderful!"

Two days later the church basement was full

of enthusiastic teenagers tackling the women's room with ladders, hats, rollers, and paint brushes. They finished in several hours and then invited the pastor in to see their handiwork.

His pleasure at the prospect of a rejuvenated washroom was suddenly cut short as he saw the color the youth had chosen—a garish purple.

"We thought we would brighten it up for them," a teenager explained proudly.

The reaction of the women was volcanic. In steady and angry succession they called the pastor. "I never saw such a hideous color in all my life!" one complained. "Those young people have ruined it."

There are no secrets in a small church, and soon the youth began getting negative vibrations from the older women. The youth were hurt. They had tried to help. They had volunteered for a job nobody else had done, but no one even said "thank you." Both sides pouted, and one old "saint" was overheard saying that children ought not to meddle in the affairs of the church. The project ended with most of the older women of the church alienated from the youth—and vice versa.

Conflict often invades the church! So there is much need for people within the Body of Christ to demonstrate the fine art of forgiveness. People outside the church expect forgiveness to be a characteristic of true Christians. So the failure of Christians to forgive each other often discredits the Gospel in the eyes of people who watch us to see whether our Christianity makes any significant difference in our daily attitudes.

In the early 1700s a young English clergyman named John Wesley came as a missionary to the American colony of Georgia. He met General Oglethorpe, governor of His Majesty's colony, and the discussion turned to some problems. A particular incident involving a troublemaker was mentioned.

"I never forgive," the general said firmly.

"Then, sir," replied Wesley, who later founded Methodism, "I hope you never sin."

Seventy Times Seven

Among other things, the church should be a laboratory where Christians learn how to forgive one another. These lessons should then be put to work in the world as testimony to the life-changing power of Jesus Christ. It can be argued, perhaps, that the greatest and most urgent need of the church is learning how to forgive.

The Scriptures provide a basic principle of forgiveness: "Then Peter came and said to Him, 'Lord, how often shall my brother sin against me and I forgive him? Up to seven times?'" Being very pleased, Peter may have gloated a little as he awaited Jesus' reply. How could the Master help but praise one so forgiving as Peter?

But to his astonishment, Jesus replied, "I do not say to you, up to seven times, but up to seventy times seven" (Matt. 18:21-22). Seventy times seven equals 490, and this, for all practical purposes, meant that Peter was to never stop forgiving his brothers.

A distinguished Lutheran expositor commented on these verses:

"The remission [of the sins of another] on the part of the wronged brother is an entirely separate thing and is not to be confused with the remission which God may grant. We must at once forgive every wrong, whether the wrongdoer repents and makes acknowledgment to us or not. That clears us. We hold nothing against the man who has wronged us. But he has his sin to settle with God." [1]

In the church today, what does it mean to forgive "seventy times seven?"

The angry women mentioned at the beginning of this chapter would, by grace, rise above their personal dislike of the peculiar color used by the teenagers. They would look beyond the "hideous" color and see the good motive of the youth. The women would smile and say, "Thanks so much"— and through God's grace they would mean it.

The teenagers? They would recognize that older people sometimes have a preference for less garish colors. And the youth would understand that their elders love the church as much as they—but perhaps in a different way. The youth might go to the older women and say, "We're sorry we went ahead without asking you what color you like. Tell us what you prefer and we'll use that."

Impossible? "With men [and women] this is impossible, but with God all things are possible" (Matt. 19:26).

For a preacher, forgiving seventy times seven means making an effort to love that layman who is "agin" everything the preacher proposes.

---

[1] R. C. H. Lenski, *The Interpretation of St. Matthew's Gospel* (Columbus, Ohio: Wartburg, 1943), p. 708.

To forgive means to love such a person *in spite of* his unlovableness. This is how God loved us. "But God demonstrates His own love toward us, in that while we were yet sinners, Christ died for us" (Rom. 5:8).

For the person in the pew, forgiving seventy times seven could mean supporting the minister even when he has some new ideas about church finances, the choir, or the ushers. And it will undoubtedly mean forgiving him when his sermon comes off poorly.

The opportunities for forgiving in any church are countless. The above suggest only a very few possibilities.

Forgiveness and Tolerance

Jesus is very clear about the difference between forgiving repeatedly, and indefinitely tolerating what is wrong. He said, "If your brother sins, go and reprove him in private; if he listens to you, you have won your brother. But if he does not listen to you, take one or two more with you, so that by the mouth of two or three witnesses every fact may be confirmed. And if he refuses to listen then, tell it to the church; and if he refuses to listen even to the church, let him be to you as a Gentile and a tax-gatherer" (Matt. 18:15-17).

Here we see an important principle which often confuses the church. To forgive someone who has sinned against you does not mean you are to accept his sin and say, "What you have done really doesn't matter." Forgiving another person means that you bear no hurt feelings, no anger, no resentment, or bitterness toward this person who wronged you.

When you personally extend forgiveness, your concern for the sinning brother's welfare may jar him loose from sin and bring him repenting to Christ for cleansing. This is the purpose of the three steps of church discipline which Jesus outlined (Matt. 18:15-17). The final step, ostracism or excommunication, shows how seriously Jesus regarded unrepentant sinners. Perhaps He was thinking of the sin of Achan, which caused God to be angry with "the sons of Israel" (Josh. 7:1). In the church, all the members are somehow affected by the sins of *one* church member. These sins must be dealt with, lest God's anger be directed against the entire church. The sobering story of Achan and his sin needs to be read and pondered by every church as a reminder to deal with sin as God wishes (Josh. 7; Matt. 18:15-17).

A biblical church is a church where people freely and unceasingly forgive one another and hold no hard feelings. But it is also a church which demands that Body members stop living in a way that displeases God. Rather than tolerate sin, the church will eventually cast out chronic, unrepentant sinners. Refusing to repent, in continued defiance of the Christian community and God's Word, means that the erring person has repudiated God's authority and is, in fact, a pagan within the community of faith.

This principle is well illustrated in the most lurid scandal reported in the New Testament. Writing to the Christians at Corinth, the Apostle Paul said,

It is actually reported that there is immorality among you, and immorality of such a kind as does not exist even among the Gentiles, that someone has his father's wife.

And you have become arrogant, and have not mourned instead, in order that the one who had done this deed might be removed from your midst.

For I, on my part, though absent in body but present in spirit, have already judged him who has so committed this, as though I were present.

In the name of our Lord Jesus, when you are assembled, and I with you in spirit, with the power of our Lord Jesus,

I have decided to deliver such a one to Satan for the destruction of his flesh, that his spirit may be saved in the day of the Lord Jesus.

Your boasting is not good. Do you not know that a little leaven leavens the whole lump of dough?

Clean out the old leaven, that you may be a new lump, just as you are in fact unleavened. For Christ our Passover also has been sacrificed.

Let us therefore celebrate the feast, not with old leaven, nor with the leaven of malice and wickedness, but with the unleavened bread of sincerity and truth.

I wrote you in my letter not to associate with immoral people.

I did not at all mean with the immoral people of this world, or with the covetous and swindlers, or with idolaters; for then you would have to go out of the world.

But actually, I wrote to you not to associate with any so-called brother if he should be an immoral person, or covetous, or an idolater, or a reviler, or a drunkard, or a swindler—not even to eat with such a one.

For what have I to do with judging outsiders? Do you not judge those who are within the church?

But those who are outside, God judges. Remove the wicked man from among yourselves. (1 Cor. 5)

The purpose of Paul's drastic discipline is clear: "I have decided to deliver such a one to Satan for the destruction of his flesh, that his spirit may be saved in the day of the Lord Jesus" (v. 5). He hopes that excommunication will lead the sinner to repentance and final salvation.

Paul also warns that the church will be infected if it tolerates continuing sin: "Do you not know that a little leaven leavens the whole lump of dough?" (v. 6). Paul's concern here is twofold: first, for the individual's ultimate welfare; second, for the welfare of the entire church. Discipline, therefore, must be carried out with care.

The Nadir of the Church

Discipline should never be self-righteous condemnation of the sinner, but all too often this is what happens. Distorted attempts to carry out the principle Paul gave to the Corinthians and the instructions Jesus gave His disciples have led the church to its poorest moments.

Loveless perversion of discipline has done infinite harm to the church. It has turned away sensitive, thinking people and has permeated popular literature with the image of Christians as narrow, self-righteous, and bigoted people. In his recent historical novel, *Centennial,* James A. Michener tells how a church in Lancaster, Pennsylvania ostracized one young man for a sin of which the boy was not really guilty:

The Mennonites decided to shun him. From that moment he became an outcast. He could not attend church, nor speak with anyone who did. He could not buy or sell, or give or take. He could converse with no man, and the idea of striking up a friendship with any woman was beyond imagination.

"They're shunnin' Levi Zent!"

"About time, that animal." [2]

What Michener describes in fiction happens all too often in fact. The loveless, "orthodox" church became for Levi Zent a monster of repulsion rather than a place of redemption, grace, and forgiveness. It intensified the boy's humiliation and simultaneously intensified the church members' smug sense of self-righteousness.

Contrary to Levi Zent's experience, the incident involving the Corinthian church member guilty of incest ended happily. The church followed Paul's orders, and apparently this was done in the right manner. In a second letter to this church Paul wrote:

But I determined this for my own sake, that I would not come to you in sorrow again.

For if I cause you to sorrow, who then makes me glad but the one whom I made sorrowful?

And this is the very thing I wrote you, lest, when I came, I should have sorrow from those who ought to make me rejoice; having confidence in you all, that my joy would be the joy of you all.

For out of much affliction and anguish of heart I wrote to you with many tears; not that you should be made sorrowful, but that you might know the love which I have especially for you.

But if any has caused sorrow, he has caused sorrow

[2] James A. Michener, *Centennial* (New York: Random House, 1974), p. 246.

not to me, but in some degree—in order not to say too much—to all of you.

Sufficient for such a one is this punishment which was inflicted by the majority, so that on the contrary you should rather forgive and comfort him, lest somehow such a one be overwhelmed by excessive sorrow.

Wherefore I urge you to reaffirm your love for him.

For to this end also I wrote that I might put you to the test, whether you are obedient in all things.

But whom you forgive anything, I forgive also; for indeed what I have forgiven, if I have forgiven anything, I did it for your sakes in the presence of Christ,

in order that no advantage be taken of us by Satan; for we are not ignorant of his schemes (2 Cor. 2:1-11).

Note how reluctant Paul was to carry out the fearsome penalty of excommunication. Knowing human nature so well, he realized how easily the affair might have ended in a carnival of self-righteousness.

Dr. Paul Tournier asked, "By what deformation has Christianity succeeded in so often crushing men instead of freeing them?"[3] Another writer asked:

If a Christian has fallen into scandalous sin, does it not, in fact, to an extent we dare not limit nor define, depend on the attitude held towards him by his fellow-believers, that is by the church, whether the realized peace of reconciliation with God will ever again be his?

If in judgment they are merciless, if they draw away their skirts from the pollution of his touch, how

---

[3] Tournier, *Guilt and Grace*, p. 54.

can he again open his heart spontaneously to the compassion of the Father? If he finds none here [in the church] who can give and receive freely the blessed experience of reconciliation, with its incalculable power to neutralize and transcend the past, will he soon believe that the Lord of heaven and earth can pardon and restore the soul? Or is it not only too likely that the pitilessness of man will hide the pity of God? [4]

A Church That Loves

Love that cares enough to make demands triumphs. We have an enduring example in the believer, lifted by the Holy Spirit to a level of redemptive discipline and effective forgiveness. This miracle was well described in the beloved hymn of John Newton: " 'Twas grace that taught my heart to fear / And grace my fears relieved."

For *fears* we might substitute the word *guilt*. Guilt, acted upon creatively by the Holy Spirit in His convicting work, does produce fears. These inner apprehensions drive the guilty one to seek the grace that relieves fear. Thus fear can lead to final assurance found in a Saviour who, by sheer grace, changes the sinner's destiny from hell to heaven, and sends the Holy Spirit to indwell and guard against sin moment by moment.

The Church is God's special instrument in the redeeming process. Through the faithful preaching, teaching, and witness of its people, the church arouses holy "fears" in the sinner, and then ex-

---

[4] H. R. Mackintosh, *The Christian Experience of Forgiveness* (London: Nisbet, 1927), p. 283-4.

emplifies God's attitude of forgiveness toward sinners.

A church without forgiveness fails to understand what God has ordained His Church to be: the example of God's grace in daily life. Thus the Church exists to provide a preview of divine forgiveness, the ultimate gift of God who was in Christ, reconciling the world to Himself (2 Cor. 5:19). This is why the Bible teaches:

"As those who have been chosen of God, holy and beloved, put on a heart of compassion, kindness, humility, gentleness and patience; bearing with one another, and forgiving each other, whoever has a complaint against any one; just as the Lord forgave you, so also should you. And beyond all these things put on love, which is the perfect bond of unity" (Col. 3:12-14).

And again: "Do not grieve the Holy Spirit of God, by whom you were sealed for the day of redemption. Let all bitterness and wrath and anger and clamor and slander be put away from you, along with all malice. And be kind to one another, tenderhearted, forgiving each other, just as God in Christ has also forgiven you" (Eph. 4:30-32).

And again: "Confess your sins to one another, and pray for one another, so that you may be healed" (James 5:16).

The Lord's Prayer also calls for forgiveness. H. A. Ironside commented:

He who is forgiven is then called upon to forgive those who sin against him. The prayer, "Forgive us our debts, as we forgive our debtors" is not a prayer from the lips of a lost sinner. It is the cry of a disciple. Forgiven eternally, the believer nevertheless needs daily forgiveness when, as an erring child of God, he grieves His Holy Spirit by allowing any unholy thing in his life and walk. And he is therefore exhorted to forgive as God in Christ has forgiven him. He who refuses to show grace to an erring brother will have to feel the rod upon his own back.[5]

It is unmistakably clear that God expects His Church to be a forgiving Body. This principle is needed to understand one of Jesus' most difficult teachings: "Truly I say to you, whatever you shall bind on earth shall have been bound in heaven; and whatever you loose on earth shall be loosed in heaven" (Matt. 18:18). Here Jesus speaks of the community of disciplined forgiveness. That is why this troublesome statement comes *after* our Lord's teaching on church discipline (vv. 15-17) but *before* His teaching about unlimited forgiveness (vv. 21-22).

Much of the Protestant Church, in a traditional reaction against ritual confession in the Roman Church, has eliminated altogether any form of confession to one another. We have no required time of confession; often our worship has no place for confession. Neither Protestant nor Roman Catholic has a right to claim superiority, for both have fallen short of God's desire in this matter.

What is the answer? To think, to ponder, to ask the Holy Spirit's guidance in making your church the laboratory of forgiveness which God wants it to be.

---

[5] Ironside, *Except Ye Repent,* pp. 141-2.

10

The Plea
for Forgiveness

Just as a mighty, snowcapped mountain towers above all other peaks in the surrounding mountain range, so does one Scripture passage seem to rise high above other Bible teachings about guilt and forgiveness. This is Psalm 51.

One Bible commentator wrote: "This psalm bears the marks of deep inner grief over sin." In the words of Osterley's statement, "For the realization of the sense of sin, set forth with unflinching candor, it has no equal." [1]

John Calvin, the great reformer, introduced his commentary on Psalm 51 with these words: "David has set an example to all such as may have sinned against God, teaching them the duty of humbly

---

[1] H. C. Leupold, *Exposition of the Psalms* (Columbus, Ohio: Wartburg, 1959), pp. 399-400.

complying with the calls to repentance, which may be addressed to them by His servants, instead of remaining under sin till they be surprised by the final vengeance of Heaven." [2]

Because of its richness and depth, Psalm 51 makes a fitting conclusion for a book about guilt and repentance in biblical perspective. For this reason the final three chapters will concentrate on this majestic Psalm.

The results of studying Psalm 51 can be surprising. Voltaire, the famous French atheist, once tired to "burlesque" Psalm 51. He began by reading it carefully to plan his satire. In the process "he became so oppressed and overawed by its solemn devotional tone that he threw down the pen and fell back half senseless on his couch, in an agony of remorse." [3]

The Structure of Psalm 51

It is helpful to begin study of any passage of Scripture by noting its structure. This is similar to a doctor examining an X ray to visualize the bone structure of his patient.

Especially useful has been the commentary of Dr. H. C. Leupold, a master expositor in the tradition of Martin Luther. His outline for Psalm 51 is a good one: [4]

A. The basic plea for pardon, vv. 1-2.

---

[2] John Calvin, (James Morrison, ed.) *Commentary on the Book of Psalms* (Grand Rapids: Eerdmans Publishing Company, n.d.), p. 282.

[3] Taylor, *David: King of Israel,* p. 273.

[4] Leupold, *Exposition of the Psalms,* p. 400.

B. The reasons on which this plea is built, vv. 3-6.

C. The plea renewed in manifold detail, vv. 13-17.

E. A prayer for the welfare of the holy city, vv. 18-19.

Historical Background

In chapter 1 we briefly mentioned King David's triple tragedy. But as we begin this study of Psalm 51, we will review it.

David was the religious and political leader of the nation Israel at its time of highest glory, about 950 years before the birth of Christ. Under David's leadership, the kingdom grew strong and prosperous. Even later, Jews would look back upon the glory of David's time. It was the high water mark for God's chosen people after their deliverance from Egypt.

But the glory of David was tarnished by David's sin. David saw Bathsheba, the wife of another man, and lusted after her. She and David committed adultery, while her husband, Uriah, was out on the battlefield fighting for King David (2 Sam. 11). Bathsheba became pregnant by King David, and he brought her husband home from the war, so it would appear that Uriah, not David, had fathered the child. But, true to the military discipline code that discouraged sexual intercourse in time of war, Uriah ignored his wife. Thus he signed his death warrant, for the desperate king schemed to have Uriah killed. He ordered that Bathsheba's husband be sent into the fighting and then left to be killed.

So Uriah died fighting for Israel, never suspecting that he had been betrayed by his wife and King David.

After Uriah's death, and after Bathsheba had mourned appropriately, King David took Bathsheba as one of his wives. This legalized, after the fact, conception of their illegitimate child. Evidently King David tried to live as if he had done nothing wrong.

Perhaps the people knew what had happened, but even if they were ignorant of the events, God was not. His relationship with King David had been broken. The Holy One of Israel could not tolerate sin—especially in the nation's anointed leader. David's beautiful psalms must have ceased, for a heart dark with guilt and sin cannot praise God until forgiveness is received and cleansing has occurred.

"Alas for him," wrote the commentator Kitto, "the bird which once rose to heights unattained before by mortal wing, filling the air with joyful songs, now lies, with maimed wing, upon the ground, pouring forth doleful cries to God." [5]

About a year passed. Then God sent the prophet Nathan to David . . .

to tell David this story: "There were two men in a certain city, one very rich, owning many flocks of sheep and herds of goats; and the other very poor, owning nothing but a little lamb he had managed to buy. It was his children's pet and he fed it from

---

[5] Taylor, *David: King of Israel*, p. 277.

his own plate and let it drink from his own cup; he cuddled it in his arms like a baby daughter. Recently a guest arrived at the home of the rich man. But instead of killing a lamb from his own flocks for food for the traveler, he took the poor man's lamb and roasted it and served it."

David was furious. "I swear by the living God," he vowed, "any man who would do a thing like that should be put to death; he shall repay four lambs to the poor man for the one he stole, and for having no pity."

Then Nathan said to David, "*You* are that rich man! The Lord God of Israel says, 'I made you king of Israel and saved you from the power of Saul. I gave you his palace and his wives and the kingdoms of Israel and Judah; and if that had not been enough, I would have given you much, much more. Why, then, have you despised the laws of God and done this horrible deed? For you have murdered Uriah and stolen his wife. Therefore murder shall be a constant threat in your family from this time on, because you have insulted me by taking Uriah's wife. I vow that because of what you have done I will cause your own household to rebel against you. I will give your wives to another man, and he will go to bed with them in public view. You did it secretly, but I will do this to you openly, in the sight of all Israel."

"I have sinned against the Lord," David confessed to Nathan.

"Then Nathan replied, "Yes, but the Lord has forgiven you, and you won't die for this sin. But you have given great opportunity to the enemies of the Lord to despise and blaspheme Him, so your child shall die."

Then Nathan returned to his home. And the Lord made Bathsheba's baby deathly sick.

(2 Sam. 12:1-15, LB)

Using Nathan as His instrument, God broke

through David's game of "I'm OK." The sorrowing king wrote a psalm to describe the impact of Nathan's words. Taylor made this perceptive comment about the sincerity of David's penitence: "An impression may be produced in a moment which will remain indelible . . . This 'Thou art the man' of Nathan's was so to him. It revealed to him, by its momentary brilliance, the full aggravation of his iniquity. He did not need or desire a second sight of it. This was enough to stir him up to hatred of his sin, and of himself." [6]

The Holy Spirit moved David to express not only the depths of his anguish, but also a marvelous faith in God's mercy. Thus Psalm 51 is a case history of a backslider's repentance.

Sin is a persistent problem for God's people, so David's psalm is always relevant. It reveals many important principles for us to grasp as we find our way back to God after we have displeased Him.

Taylor ends his study of David's "The Great Transgression" with these thoughts:

If even a David fell so fearfully, who among us can be secure? Here was a man of preeminent ability, of great piety, and of extensive usefulness, and yet he was guilty of the most revolting sin. Surely the practical inference is, "Let him that thinketh he standeth take heed lest he fall" (1 Cor. 10:12). No station in society, no eminence in the church, no excellence in character, no more inspiration of genius can keep a man from sin; nay, not even the gift of

---

[6] Taylor, *David: King of Israel*, p. 272.

divine inspiration can preserve its possessor from a fall. Nothing can do that but the grace of God working in him through prayer, and persevering watchfulness. I say persevering watchfulness, for our vigilance must be continued so long as life on earth shall last.[7]

From this background, we turn now to Psalm 51 itself.

1. Be gracious to me, O God, according to Thy loving-kindness; according to the greatness of Thy compassion blot out my transgressions.

How do you begin a conversation with One whom you have wronged? One from whom you have been trying to conceal the ugly truth? One who has loved you in the past and chose you for high honor? One who already knows your dreadful secret but waits for you to bring the matter up and seek His forgiveness?

The Holy Spirit led David to begin, not by pouring out a recital of his sins. Rather, David began his confession with a statement of faith about the One from whom David sought forgiveness and cleansing. The nature of God is the proper starting place of all true prayer. The Lord's Prayer (Matt. 6:9-13), for example, begins by focusing upon God's holiness. So it should be in prayers of confession, for everything depends upon the nature of the One who forgives. Is He hard? Is He resentful? Is He stingy with His forgiveness? Or is He known to be merciful?

---

[7] Taylor, *David: King of Israel*, p. 278.

Through the years before his great sin, David had learned that God is amazingly kind. When a new king was needed to replace unfaithful, demented Saul, God passed over many strong and intelligent men who may have been well-qualified to be the human leader of God's people. Instead, He chose David, a sweet-voiced shepherd boy, youngest of Jesse's sons and the most unlikely candidate of all.

God's election of David was a mystery of loving-kindness. So he wrote from personal experience when he began his confession by mentioning God's mercy and loving-kindness.

What sort of God will you call upon when it comes time for your confession? A God of mercy and compassion? Or do you imagine God to be petty? Vindictive? Do you think He is watching, waiting to condemn you for every little mistake you make?

Many people want forgiveness, but their too-small God lacks the capacity to forgive. The tragedy is that these are often church people, "religious" folks who read their Bibles, pray faithfully, and sit in church twice a week. But this activity is to no avail because they have not realized that God is merciful and kind. Deep in their hearts they don't really expect to receive forgiveness.

David had had a long, personal relationship with God. His sin with Bathsheba had built a wall of guilt between him and God. But his confession was not the first contact between them, and David knew God was a God of mercy and compassion.

Your relationship with God is a bridge over

which you may come to Him any time. A fool fails to build a bridge till it is needed; a wise man builds the bridge before he must cross over it. This bridge to God is built through daily obedience, prayer, praise, worship, giving thanks in all circumstances, and getting familiar with His Word, the Bible.

"Blot out my transgressions," David pleaded. His plea for forgiveness is predictive, for it pointed ahead to Christ, who was the answer to that prayer —and to the plea of every other sinner. It was God's deliberate will and plan for His only Son to die in order to blot out the sins of all who would accept His sacrificial death as payment for their own sins.

2. *Wash me thoroughly from my iniquity, and cleanse me from my sin.*

David was not seeking a partial cleanup—he asked to be made thoroughly clean. That is often a deep yearning in the human heart—to be set entirely free from sin's foulness—from the guilt that clings—from the ungodliness that lurks in the hidden cellars of the heart (Jer. 17:9; Matt. 15:19).

Here is another evidence of genuine repentance: the repentant seeks *total* cleansing. Many people stumble at this crucial point. They want only a partial cure. They want the unpleasant effects of their sins to be removed, *but they have no real desire that the source of sin be cleansed entirely.* Pain causes them to seek relief for symptoms, but not the cure of the disease itself.

"Lord make me chaste—but not yet," Augustine prayed when he was a young man with a mistress and illegitimate child. God was pulling the future Christian leader toward repentance. He realized that a change in his immoral life-style would be required, but he was not ready to give up his mistress.

Earlier (chapter 3), we talked about a minister who was burdened with guilt because he had cheated during a Greek examination in seminary. For years, guilt weighed heavily on his heart. But when an obvious answer was suggested by a counselor, the minister drew back; he did not want total cleansing, he only wanted relief from the uncomfortableness of his guilt. He backed away from entire cleansing as from a live rattlesnake.

Yet God demands total purity, complete cleanness. Jesus said, "You [disciples] are to be perfect, as your heavenly Father is perfect" (Matt. 5:48). Perfect as God? That means every speck of impurity removed. That means to "wash yourselves, make yourselves clean; remove the evil of your deeds from My sight. . . . Though your sins are as scarlet, they will be white as snow; though they are red like crimson, they will be like wool" (Isa. 1:16, 18).

Any lingering doubts about God's desire for our full purification should be removed by these words: "Now may the God of peace Himself *sanctify you entirely;* and may your spirit and soul and body be preserved complete, without blame at the coming of our Lord Jesus Christ" (1 Thes. 5:23).

Christians generally interpret this verse in one of two different ways. Some believe this entire cleansing, or completed sanctification, happens only after death, in eternity. In this life, they say, believers are "going on *toward* perfection," but it will not be achieved this side of the grave.

Others believe that God intends our sanctification to be entire in this life. Christ, by His indwelling, cleanses the believer's desires and motives so he can love God entirely and love his neighbor as much as self. The sanctified believer will make many mistakes, but the intent of his heart will be without sin.

Whatever position on "sanctification" individual Christians take, all agree that a yearning after purity, such as King David expressed (Psalm 51), is the mark of one who really loves God and who is moving ahead, by God's grace, toward God's perfect will.

Why does David ask for cleansing?

3. For I know my transgressions, and my sin is ever before me.

No trace of excuse can be found here. David did not play games with God, pretending he had not really sinned or blaming someone else. Here is another mark of genuine repentance: facing the wrong honestly. The spirit of honesty is evident in David's frank admission of sin.

Many times we would prefer to call our transgressions "mistakes." But, are these the same? Guilt has about it a haunting quality. "My sin is *ever before me*," David wrote. John Calvin commented:

From [David's] example we may learn who are they that can alone be said to seek reconciliation with God in a proper manner. They are such as have had their conscience wounded with a sense of sin, and who can find no rest until they have obtained assurance of His mercy. We will never seriously apply to God for pardon, until we have obtained such a view of our sins as inspires us with fear. The more easily satisfied we are under our sins, the more we provoke God to punish them with severity. And if we really desire absolution from His hand, we must do more than confess our guilt in words; we must institute a rigid and formidable scrutiny into the character of our transgressions.[8]

4a. Against Thee, Thee only, I have sinned, and done what is evil in Thy sight.

What an amazing statement! David had lusted after another man's wife and committed adultery with her; she became pregnant. Then he had schemed to get Bathsheba's husband killed in battle. Finally, he had pretended for a while that in all this he had done no wrong.

The list of the sinned-against included Bathsheba, Uriah, and the nation. How then could David say that he had sinned only against God?

Consider a bank robbery. The theft involves not only the teller who was threatened at gunpoint, but the bank officers, the bystanders, and the bank stockholders are all affected by the sin in one way or another.

Similarly, every sin is against God. There is no such thing as sin which affects only you or only other people. Always sin affects God. He created the whole universe; He set it in motion ac-

---

[8] Calvin, *Commentary,* pp. 284-5.

cording to His moral and physical laws. Any sin is a displacing, a setting aside of the law, the will, and the purposes of God. Any sin against a part is a sin against the whole. If you slice my finger with a knife, you wound not only my finger, but you wound *me*.

Jesus helps us understand this in His preview of what will happen at the Last Judgment: "Truly I say to you, to the extent that you did it to one of these brothers of Mine, even the least of them, you did it to Me" (Matt. 25:40). To give clothing to a prisoner, forgotten in a jail cell, is to show kindness to that prisoner and to *Christ Himself*. To give a drink of water to a thirsty person is to give a drink to Christ.

What God made is a part of Himself; to touch His creation is, somehow, to touch Him who made and sustains all things.

At the Last Judgment, Jesus will explain to the damned that they are going to hell for eternity because they failed to understand that responsibility to God cannot be separated from responsibility to His creatures (Matt. 25:41-46). A sin against another human being is a sin against God Himself.

Humanists, obsessed with "social concern," talk as if sin has only the human dimension. They resemble a man who sees with only one eye. They lose true biblical perspective of sin because they do not have a God-dimension in their understanding of sin. By downgrading the Scriptures, especially the Old Testament, they overlook the tremendous truth which the Holy Spirit revealed to David: that every sin is, ultimately, a sin against God.

Sin against God can only be counterbalanced on the scales of eternity by a compensating sacrifice made by God Himself. No lesser sacrifice can atone for transgression against God.

Every sin, therefore, is deadly serious. Every sin of your tongue. Every sin of your imagination. Every sin created by what you failed to do. Every sin resulting from what you did. All are transgressions against the holy love and majesty of the living God.

When this idea comes to us, we must declare with young Isaiah, "Woe is me, for I am ruined! Because I am a man of unclean lips, and I live among a people of unclean lips, for my eyes have seen the King, the Lord of hosts" (Isa. 6:5).

What is "evil in [God's] sight?" This is not always easy to know. Some who watched Jesus' crucifixion thought it was only "evil." What else was the death of the One whom they knew as the Son of God, the One who had blessed and healed multitudes? That He should die nailed to a cross, like the worst criminals, *had* to be evil!

But gradually, by faith, the followers of Jesus recognized that His death, though carried out by evil men, had accomplished good rather than evil; His death would bring eternal life to millions.

One reason God gave us the Scriptures is that we might know what is "evil" in His sight. And that knowing this, we might avoid the wide way that leads to destruction and walk, instead, "in a manner worthy of the calling with which [we]

have been called, with all humility and gentleness, with patience, showing forbearance to one
another in love" (Eph. 4:1-2).

The Holy Spirit makes our consciences sensitive.
He warns us when we are wrong and when we
are right in God's sight. The Apostle Paul wrote,
"The Spirit Himself bears witness with our spirits
that we are children of God" (Rom. 8:16). We will
prefer to do good. Then we can be sure that God
will cause "all things to work together for good
to those who love God, to those who are called
according to His purpose" (Rom. 8:28).

*4b. So that Thou art justified when Thou dost
speak, and blameless when Thou dost judge.*

David makes an open admission of sin. Making
no excuses, he acknowledges the perfect right God
has to judge him guilty. The creature acknowledges
the superior right of the Creator.

Many Christians stumble on this point. They
are not willing to "let God be God." Instead, they
place their own free will ahead of God's sovereign
power over their lives. Thus many Christians, professing a Bible faith, shrink God down to a size
where they can "control" Him rather than He
controlling them.

They protest, "If God controls me, I would only
be a puppet and God would pull the strings!" This,
supposedly, is the objection to end all objections
to control by an all-powerful God.

Do you believe that God is all-wise, all-good?
That He is perfect and just in every respect? That
He never makes a mistake? If you believe this, then

it should be sheer joy for you to be a "puppet" in His hands. A God who has shown what He is like in Jesus Christ can be trusted. To be His puppet—to move only as He willed—would be unspeakable joy.

In his confession, King David sets aside all claims to control over his life. Why not? With David in control, life had become a snakepit of lechery, murder, and deception. Faced, in a moment of truth, with his pitiful inadequacy, David conceded his authority to God. David moved upward from utter depravity to a higher state of godliness than he had previously known. The key was his full surrender into the hands of God, the Holy One, who has every right to say and do what He pleases.

Lest some argue that this is a concept unique to the Old Testament, consider again Paul's words, given by the same Holy Spirit who guided David: "Who are you, O man, who answers back to God? The thing molded will not say to the molder, 'Why did you make me like this,' will it?" (Rom. 9:20).

Unwillingness to surrender all to God keeps many Christians in bondage to sin. They will not acknowledge that He is better able to manage their lives than they. We are only playing at religion until we say, in deepest love, "Father, make me Your puppet. Let my hands, my feet, and my mind, move only at the impulse of Your love."

5. Behold, I was brought forth in iniquity, and in sin my mother conceived me.

Usually, people think that sin is something you *do*—rob banks, cheat on your income tax, or sleep with somebody else's wife. *Actions* are seen as sin in our action-oriented society.

But here David reveals another great truth: *Sin is what I am.* The innate depravity of my whole self causes individual acts of sin. Jesus expressed it this way: "The things that proceed out of the mouth come from the heart, and those defile the man. For out of the heart come evil thoughts, murders, adulteries, fornications, thefts, false witness, slanders" (Matt. 15:18-19). An act of sin is the symptom of sin—as the itching red rash is a symptom of measles.

It is human nature to resist admitting that we have committed sinful acts; even more do we resist fiercely the truth: "I *am* sin." Admitting this emphasizes the great gulf between God and His fallen creatures. Yet this is what King David confessed when he said, "I was brought forth in iniquity, in sin my mother conceived me."

Humanism has emasculated the Bible's teaching of total depravity, minimizing the rottenness of human nature apart from redemption in and through Christ. No wonder that evangelism and missions languish where church people feel they are good enough in and of themselves to merit God's love.

Strangely, this has happened with acceleration during the 20th century—a period which has seen two great world wars, plus countless lesser wars, uprisings and revolutions. In this "enlightened century," social evils have multiplied beyond control.

The illusion of human goodness went up in the smoke of the Nazi crematories. Recent history forces an objective person to acknowledge that the Bible was correct all along. Fallen human nature is *not* "good." Rather, it is as the Apostle Paul described it:

> Realize this, that in the last days difficult times will come. For men will be lovers of self, lovers of money, boastful, arrogant, revilers, disobedient to parents, ungrateful, unholy, unloving, irreconcilable, malicious gossips, without self-control, brutal, haters of good, treacherous, reckless, conceited, lovers of pleasure rather than lovers of God; holding to a form of godliness, although they have denied its power (2 Tim. 3:1-5).

In his letter to the Romans, Paul also wrote a detailed description of degenerate human nature (3:9-18).

Why be so negative? Why emphasize human *badness?* Until we recognize and confess our sin-caused separation from God, we shall never seek Him who alone can save and sanctify. John Wesley once stated that it is impossible for anyone to be a Christian without accepting the doctrine of original sin. If the doctrine of original sin is not true, then the death of Christ was not really necessary and no one is really lost in sin. The death of Christ then was just a tragic accident and the Bible is false.

6. Behold, Thou dost desire truth in the innermost being, and in the hidden part Thou wilt make me know wisdom.

The "heart" is the inner self. Here, Jesus said, is the source of every uncleanness which shows itself in symptoms of outward sin (Matt. 15:18-19). This is not the way God made us in the beginning. Truth—"original righteousness"—lay in the hearts of Adam and Eve. But the "original sin" of Adam and Eve, recorded in Genesis 3, forever changed humanity. The original disobedience to God somehow opened the door to sin that took control of human nature. Since Adam and Eve, sin has ruled constantly, proudly enthroned in each human heart.

How can sin be *de*throned and truth *en*throned once more? How can Satan be removed from the throne and Jesus Christ coronated as Lord of one's life?

The answer is the great redemption which God has planned, centering on the atoning death and the resurrection of Jesus Christ.

Part of the Old Testament—Psalms, Proverbs, Ecclesiastes, and Song of Solomon—is known as "wisdom literature." The writers extolled wisdom as a great virtue, but the Apostle Paul explained that Jesus Christ "became to us wisdom from God, and righteousness and sanctification and redemption" (1 Cor. 1:30).

God was not content to have personified Wisdom remain a part of the past. God therefore ordained that His Wisdom should take the throne of each human life, displacing Satan who ruled there as a result of the fall of Adam. So the New Testament brings good news of an indwelling Christ. He brings the very wisdom of God down to rule over our emotions, desires, and motives. This is the heart of Paul's soul-lifting prayer for the Christians in Ephesus: "I bow my knees before the Father, from whom every family in heaven and on earth derives its name, that He would grant you, according to the riches of His glory, to be strengthened with power through His Spirit in the inner man; *so that Christ may dwell in your hearts* through faith, and that you, being rooted and grounded in love, may be able to comprehend with all the saints what is the breadth and length and height and depth, and to know the love of Christ which surpasses knowledge, that you may be filled up to all the fulness of God" (Eph. 3:14-19).

11

The Plea and Resolution

After David pleads for forgiveness, he renews his plea and resolves to honor God in speech and action.

7. Purify me with hyssop, and I shall be clean; Wash me, and I shall be whiter than snow.

Hyssop is an herb that was specified to be used in rituals for purification rights for lepers and those stricken with deadly plague. He asked God for the radical cleansing needed to match the awfulness of his sins.

Again this reveals David's honesty. He played no game with God, minimizing his transgression. This verse also reveals David's complete faith in God's cleansing ability. Cleansing from leprosy and plague—and sin—would require a miracle. David's words pointed ahead to Christ, who healed lepers

(Matt. 8:1-4; Mark 1:40-45; Luke 5:12-16; 17:11-19).

Long after David's time, the Prophet Isaiah, foretelling the atoning work of Christ upon the cross, predicted that "by His scourging we are healed" (Isa. 53:5). In one sense, this refers to healing the breach separating a holy God from sinners—healing the sickness of their sin, whose wages is death everlasting. Many also consider this verse a promise of divine healing.

8. Make me to hear joy and gladness. Let the bones which Thou has broken rejoice.

Joy is the first casualty of sin. All that remains of gladness in fellowship with God are ashes.

Taylor describes what sin did to David:

Henceforth he is no longer the man he was. He goes about crushed in spirit, humiliated before his people, and degraded even in his own estimation. The nobler features of his character seem to have become eclipsed; and the infirmities of temper, weakness of will, and even dimness of judgment, begin to appear. The spring of his life seems to have gone. The elasticity and bounce of his character are seen no more. He trusts, indeed, in God to the last, but it is not with the joyful confidence of one who is rich in the consciousness of his father's complacency, but rather with the dull and heavy grasp of one who knows that he has deeply wounded his father's heart.[1]

Such are the effects of sin. Not only is the soul distressed, but the body may also suffer as a result of guilt.

---

[1] Taylor, *David: King of Israel,* pp. 276-7.

Dr. Paul Tournier, distinguished psychiatrist, observed:

> The clinical experiences of which we have heard in our conferences show the enormous part played by the feelings of guilt in the destiny of our patients, in the emergence of many illnesses and in the failure of much treatment. Open your eyes! and you will see among your patients that huge crowd of wounded, distressed, crushed men and women, laden with secret guilts, real or false, definite or vague; even a sort of guilt at being alive, which is more common than we think.[2]

The Prophet Isaiah wrote, "Your iniquities have made a separation between you and your God and your sins have hid His face from you, so that He does not hear. . . . Therefore . . . we hope for light, but behold, darkness; for brightness but we walk in gloom. We grope along the wall like blind men, we grope like those who have no eyes; we stumble at midday as in the twilight, among those who are vigorous we are like dead men" (Isa. 59:2, 9-10).

A hint of this can be seen in the experience of Adam, the first man. He heard "the Lord God walking in the garden in the cool of the day." Ordinarily this would have been a time of closeness between God and the chief glory of His creation, Adam and Eve. But they had disobeyed. Guilt caused them to hide "themselves from the presence of the Lord God among the trees of the garden" (Gen. 3:8).

---

[2] Tournier, *Guilt and Grace,* p. 60.

Adam is every man. Guilt over our sinful acts and our sin nature make us want to hide from God. Some hide in their work. Others hide in their hobbies. Many escape through TV, other entertainment, or sex. Still others escape each weekend into gardens and cottages. Some even escape into religion where church work or theology can become a substitute for fellowship with God.

Yet underneath, all except the hopelessly hardened of heart yearn to know God personally, with the "spirit of adoption as sons by which we cry out 'Abba! Father'" (Rom. 8:15).

Speaking to God of "bones" which He had broken, David meant the emotionally crushing weight of guilt from his accumulation of unforgiven sins. The Bible also records instances where God sent some malady, so this verse may mean either physical or emotional brokenness.

Take inventory: How is your health? Consider the bone-breaking power of guilt. Then turn in repentance. Confess your sins to the Great Physician, whom David described in these words:

Bless the Lord, O my soul;
And all that is within me bless His holy name.
Bless the Lord, O my soul,
And forget none of His benefits;
Who pardons all your iniquities;
Who heals all your diseases;
Who redeems your life from the pit;
Who crowns you with loving-kindness and compassion;
Who satisfies your years with good things
So that your youth is renewed like the eagle.
(Ps. 103:1-5).

9. *Hide Thy face from my sins, and blot out all my iniquities.*

It seems that David has come full circle and is now repeating what he asked at the beginning. Why should this repetition be necessary? Was King David repeating himself in prayer simply to impress God? And why did he continue praying as if pardon had not been granted? Nathan had said to David, "The Lord has taken away your sin; you shall not die" (2 Sam. 12:13). Did David's continued pleading mean that he did not believe that God had really forgiven him?

John Calvin makes this helpful observation:

There is no reason to be surprised that David should have once again renewed his prayers for pardon, the more to confirm his belief in it. The truth is, that we cannot properly pray for pardon of sin until we have come to a persuasion that God will be reconciled to us. Who can venture to open his mouth in God's presence unless he be firmly assured of His fatherly favor? And pardon being the first thing we should pray for, it is plain that there is no inconsistency in having a persuasion of the grace of God, and yet in proceeding to supplicate His forgiveness.

In proof of this, I might refer to the Lord's Prayer, in which we are taught to begin by addressing God as our Father, and yet afterwards to pray for remission of our sins.

God's pardon is full and complete; but our faith cannot take in His overflowing goodness, and it is necessary that it should distill to us drop by drop. It is owing to this infirmity of our faith, that we are often found repeating and repeating again the same petition, not with the view surely of gradually softening the heart of God to compassion, but because we advance by slow and difficult steps to the requisite fulness of assurance.[3]

"Vain repetition" in prayer, which Jesus warned against (Matt. 6:7), is throwing up a barrage of words, believing the sheer volume will make God listen. Also, it is the mechanical repetition of prayers which you don't really mean. One of the great pitfalls in public worship is failure to mean the prayers we say or to affirm in our hearts the words of those who lead us in public prayer. John Calvin observed that the greatest blasphemy of all is repeating the Lord's Prayer automatically, without meaning it.

If you deeply desire forgiveness, and if you plead with God for His mercy and pardon, repetition such as David's can be pleasing to God because it is the genuine cry of your heart. Jesus urged persistence in prayer (Luke 11:5-10). And God honored Abraham's persistent pleading on behalf of the doomed and degenerate city of Sodom (Gen. 18:23-33).

10. Create in me a clean heart, O God, and renew a steadfast spirit within me.

David repeats his plea for cleansing. This urgency comes as a result of his recognition (v. 5) that his nature is sin, and that from this corrupted fountainhead flowed his sins of adultery and murder.

Heart-cleansing is God's specialty, for He is "not

---

[3] Calvin, *Commentary*, p. 296.

wishing for any to perish but for all to come to repentance" (2 Peter 3:9).

Jeremiah prophesied a time when "I [God] will give them a heart to know Me, for I am the Lord; and they will be My people, and I will be their God, for they will return to Me with their whole heart" (Jer. 24:7). Only the clean heart, which David requested and Jeremiah foretold, allows people to belong to God without reservation or fear.

Ezekiel pointed ahead to the New Covenant, when the atoning death and the indwelling of Christ would transform the hearts of all who welcomed Him as Saviour and Lord. Speaking prophetically through Ezekiel, God said, "I will give you a new heart, and put a new spirit within you; and I will remove the heart of stone from your flesh and give you a heart of flesh. And I will put My Spirit within you and cause you to walk in My statutes, and you will be careful to observe My ordinances" (Ezek. 36:26-27).

By asking for renewal of a "steadfast spirit," David recognized his own terrible inclination to do evil. So with a kind of terror he begged God for the gift of persevering faith and unwavering obedience.

11. Do not cast me away from Thy presence, and do not take Thy Holy Spirit from me.

Here the prayer reaches the depths of David's dread. For one who has known God and has been close to Him, no punishment could be more horrible than being "cast away from Thy presence."

And nothing could be worse than for God to withdraw His Holy Spirit.

Many Christians believe that a person whom God has chosen for salvation is among His elect and cannot, therefore, ever "fall away," that God will under no circumstances withdraw His Spirit from a believer. From this perspective, David's words constitute the frightening question: Am I really one of God's elect? Or has my profession all these years been a counterfeit? What if I am *not* among God's chosen?

Continued separation from God because of David's sin and the final withdrawal of His Holy Spirit would have meant that David's faith had never been real and that now the game was over.

Other Christians interpret this verse differently. They believe that God has elected to save all people, but that many who accept His redemption misuse their freedom, reject God, discard His salvation, and choose to live without Him. A person who is saved can, they say, "fall from grace" and be eternally lost.

In this view, the normal question asked by any godly person who had fallen into sin is: "Does this mean I have lost my salvation? Does this mean that because I have disobeyed God so flagrantly that though once I was found, now I am lost?"

Whatever position one takes, it can be said that this verse represents a statement of David's deep, haunting fear: that perhaps he has passed the point of no return with God as Saul had done earlier.

Any fall into sin should cause a believer to be

deeply concerned. It is a terrible mistake to assume that God will not tire of one's disobedience. The writer of Hebrews explained that persistent, flagrant, disobedience provoked God's anger so that He said they wouldn't enter into His rest (Heb. 3:16-17).

12. Restore to me the joy of Thy salvation, and sustain me with a willing spirit.

David's awful fear of divine rejection is followed immediately by a plea to be restored into God's good graces—and for a cooperative spirit that will cause David to bend as the will of God directs.

As we have already noted, the joy of closeness with God departs when sin comes between a believer and God. That is why Adam and Eve covered themselves and hid in the Garden after they had disobeyed God's commands. First they lost the joy of innocence; then they lost the joy of walking and talking in the garden with the heavenly Father. David had also lost his joy.

"The fact that [David] so urgently prays for a joyful heart indicates how seriously depressed he must have been," comments Dr. Leupold, "and how well aware he was of the fact that the state of grace is a state of joyfulness of heart and mind." [4]

Charles H. Spurgeon observed:

> None but God can give back this joy; He can do it; we may ask for it; He will do it for His own glory and our benefit. This joy comes not first but follows pardon and purity: in such order it is safe, in any other it is vain presumption or idiotic delirium.[5]

---

[4] Leupold, *Exposition of the Psalms*, p. 405.

Why do so many in the church lack joy? Why do some people sing the most glorious hymns and look as if they were sucking lemons? The absence of joy often betrays some barrier that is blocking off the proper relationship with God. Godly "joy," however, is more than frothy happiness and toothpaste-commercial smiles, which some Christians mistake for the real thing. Godly joy is the deep inner confidence that "in all these things we overwhelmingly conquer through Him who loved us. For I am convinced that neither death, nor life, nor angels, nor principalities, nor things present, nor things to come, nor powers, nor height, nor depth, nor any other created thing, shall be able to separate us from the love of God, which is in Christ Jesus our Lord" (Rom. 8:37-39).

Such joy is not mere sentiment; it is the serenity with which the joy-ful person faces life. Joy is not the main goal of true Christians, but rather a blessed bonus which the God of all joy gives to those who really belong to Him.

The "willing spirit" David prays for is one which inclines itself toward God. It prefers His way over the ways of the depraved and disobedient world. This "willing spirit" recognizes that the only worthwhile treasures are in heaven. So the "willing spirit" naturally seeks first God's kingdom and His righteousness.

13. Then I will teach transgressors Thy ways, and sinners will be converted to Thee.

---

[5] Charles H. Spurgeon, *The Treasury of David,* Vol. 2 (New York: Funk & Wagnalls, 1881), p. 454.

David had recognized that he could not serve God until he had been cleansed and given a "willing spirit." Only then could he become a useful instrument in God's hands, a tool for the conversion of sinners.

A great truth is given here. If we would lead others to personal knowledge of God, then we must have first gone through the purifying fires of repentance to receive a spirit willing to "seek first His kingdom and His righteousness" (Matt. 6:33). Without this, we are as useless as a chipped chisel in the hands of the carpenter. Without spirits submissive to God and willing to work His way, we may do God's cause more harm than good.

The word *then* is a hinge. On it swings the outworking of David's repentance. All that has gone before has been preparation; now the prayer leads David into future service. It is something like Isaiah's response after his cleansing in the Temple: "Here am I. Send me!" (Isa. 6:8).

Someone has said, "We are saved to serve." That is the thought which now enters David's prayer. He wants not only forgiveness, but he wants to be restored to usefulness in God's army. Forced by his sin to sit on the sidelines, David now wants to get back into the game.

True repentance never comes with a feeling of self-satisfaction at personal cleansing. Rather, gratitude for God's mercy and "another chance," thrusts one out into God's service. If you don't *want* to serve God, to be His representative and do His work wherever He has placed you, then one may question the sincerity of your repentance.

The response of the forgiven sinner is what St. Francis of Assisi expressed in a famous prayer: "Lord, make me an instrument of Thy peace. . . ."

14. Deliver me from bloodguiltiness, O God, Thou God of my salvation: then my tongue will joyfully sing of Thy righteousness.

David's tongue, set free from the paralyzing effect of guilt, freely and naturally witnesses to God's goodness.

True witness must focus on the righteousness of God. But all too often our "witnessing" finds other emphases, such as *my* experience, or what God has done for *me*. These may be useful as supplementary points of emphasis, but the main thrust of witnessing must feature God's righteousness— freely available in Christ to those who accept Him.

That is the real Good News of Christianity.

15. O Lord, open my lips that my mouth may declare Thy praise.

Here David reveals something else important about speaking for God: it happens at His initiative. He gives His servants the right words to say. Furthermore, He also arranges the opportunities for witness, bringing to us those people with whom He wishes us to work.

Realizing this frees a Christian from preoccupation with gimmicks and techniques for "soul-winning." Your job is to be sensitive enough so you will catch God's signals and then, under direction of the Holy Spirit, take advantage of the opportunity He has created. Techniques can be helpful, but only if they are subject to creative modification as the Spirit directs in each new situation. To become a prisoner of witnessing techniques guarantees artificiality.

16-17. For Thou dost not delight in sacrifice, otherwise I would give it: thou art not pleased with burnt offerings. The sacrifices of God are a broken spirit; A broken and a contrite heart, O God, Thou wilt not despise.

This is the climax of Psalm 51. Here David gives the nub of what constitutes true repentance. But first he tells what repentance is not—this is as important as knowing the nature of true repentance.

Many people feel they can pay for their sins by *doing* something, *giving* something, or *saying* something. Thus we often try to make our own atonement for sin. This did not work for the Jews, who offered elaborate ritual sacrifices as prescribed in God's Law. The author of Hebrews, speaking of the failure of Jewish ritual sacrifice, wrote: "For if the blood of goats and bulls and the ashes of a heifer sprinkling those who have been defiled, sanctify for the cleansing of the flesh, how much more will the blood of Christ, who through the eternal Spirit offered Himself without blemish to God, cleanse your conscience from dead works to serve the living God?" (Heb. 9:13:14).

God was not pleased with Jewish ritual sacrifices because most of the time they were nothing more than a form. They were the symbol of repentance (sacrifice), unaccompanied by sorrow over sin or true desire to turn away from sin.

The Old Testament prophet Micah warned God's people that ritual alone was fruitless, for God wanted something deeper than the *form* of repentance: "With what shall I come to the Lord and bow myself before God on high? Shall I come to Him with burnt offerings, with yearling calves? Does the Lord take delight in thousands of rams, in ten thousand rivers of oil? Shall I present my first-born for my rebellious acts, the fruit of my body for the sin of my soul? He has told you, O man, what is good; and what does the Lord require of you but to do justice, to love kindness, and to walk humbly with your God?" (Micah 6:6-8).

The fulfillment of God's requirements can come only from a heart set free from the values of the world, a heart dramatically changed by God to place first importance upon those qualities of God's eternal Kingdom: justice, kindness, humility, and closeness to God. But this heart comes about by first being broken.

What is the "broken and contrite heart" David mentions? The description of such a heart has been magnificently given throughout this psalm. In all the Bible there is no better example. The confessional part of David's psalm ends with a statement of faith that God will not despise, scorn, reject, or ignore the humbled. Jesus also said, "Blessed are the poor in spirit, for theirs is the kingdom of heaven" (Matt. 5:3). The Apostle Peter wrote, "Humble yourselves, therefore, under the mighty hand of God, that He may exalt you at the proper time, casting all your anxiety upon Him, because He cares for you" (1 Peter 5:6-7).

18-19. By Thy favor do good to Zion; build the walls of Jerusalem. Then Thou wilt delight in righteous sacrifices, In burnt offering and whole burnt offering; then young bulls will be offered on Thy altar.

It seems as if these verses are "tacked on," but they form a proper ending. At the last, David shifts from intense concentration on his personal sin and its forgiveness to the welfare of his nation. Leupold comments:

> [So far] the psalm . . . has said nothing as to the possible effect that David's sin may have had upon the whole nation. Yet it is unthinkable that after his recovery David should not have felt what his wicked example might do to his people. It is equally unthinkable that he should not have prayed to God to turn aside the evil effects of his bad example.[6]

God's people have a sacred obligation to pray for their rulers—and rulers should pray for the people and nation over which God has placed them (Rom. 13:1). David's closing words show his desire to repair the damage he had caused.

Perhaps David ended this psalm of confession hoping that the nation might follow his good example of a "broken and contrite heart" rather than following his bad example of adultery, murder, and pretense. He prayed that the city would continue growing, in spite of what had happened; he asked God's blessing upon Jerusalem. In faith, David looked ahead to the time when God would reign

---

[6] Leupold, *Exposition on the Psalms*, p. 408.

in every heart, when sacrifice would not just be an empty ritual, but the symbol of sorrow over sin and trust for God's forgiveness.

Bibliography

Augustin (A. C. Coxe, ed). *Exposition on the Book of Psalms*. Grand Rapids: Eerdmans, 1956.

Benson, George A. *Then Joy Breaks Through*. New York: Seabury Press, 1972.

Berne, Eric. *Games People Play*. New York: Grove Press, 1964.

Bookwalter, Lewis. *Repentance*. Dayton, Ohio: United Brethren Publishing House, 1902.

Calvin, John (James Anderson, ed.) *Commentary on the Book of Psalms* (vol. 2). Grand Rapids: Eerdmans, n.d.

Colquhoun, John, *Repentance*. London: Banner of Truth Trust, 1965 (1832).

Counts, Bill and Narramore, Bruce. *Guilt and Freedom*. Irvine, Ca.: Harvest House, 1974.

Davidson, Francis, ed. *The New Bible Commentary*. Grand Rapids: Eerdmans, 1953.

Douglas, J. D., ed. *The New Bible Dictionary*. Grand Rapids: Eerdmans, 1962.

Emerson, James G., Jr. *The Dynamics of Forgiveness*. Philadelphia: Westminster, 1964.

Ironside, H. A. *Except Ye Repent*. Grand Rapids: Zondervan Publishing House, 1972.

Kay, J. Alan, ed. *Fifty Hymns by Charles Wesley*. London: Epworth Press, 1957.

Lenski, R. C. H. *The Interpretation of St. Matthew's Gospel.* Columbus, Ohio: Wartburg, 1943.

Leupold, H. C. *Exposition of The Psalms.* Columbus, Ohio: Wartburg, 1959.

Mackintosh, H. R. *The Christian Experience of Forgiveness.* London: Nisbet, 1927.

Menninger, Karl. *Whatever Became of Sin?* New York: Hawthorn Books, 1973.

Michener, James A. *Centennial.* New York: Random House, 1974.

Morrison, James Dalton, ed. *Masterpieces of Religious Verse.* New York: Harper Brothers Publishers, 1948.

Redlich, E. Basil. *The Forgiveness of Sins.* Edinburgh: T. T. Clark, 1937.

Scott, R. B. Y. *The Psalms as Christian Praise.* New York: Association Press, 1958.

Spurgeon, C. H. *The Treasury of David* (vol. 2). New York: Funk & Wagnalls, 1881.

Taylor, William H. *David: King of Israel.* New York: Harper, 1876.

Telfer, W. *The Forgiveness of Sins.* Philadelphia: Muhlenberg, 1960.

Tournier, Paul. *Guilt and Grace.* New York: Harper & Row, 1958.

Walden, Treadwell. *The Great Meaning of Matanoia, an undeveloped chapter in the Life and Teaching of Christ.* New York: Thomas Whittaker, 1896.

Inspirational Victor Books for Your Enjoyment

Inspirational Victor Books for Your Enjoyment

BE REAL An excellent practical and devotional study of 1 John, by Warren W. Wiersbe. Rich in illustrations that guide students in applying truths to their living. Textbook **6-2046—$1.75**/Leader's Guide **6-2902—95¢**

THE GOOD LIFE A study of the Epistle of James, by Henry Jacobsen. Acquaints students with God's plan of salvation, and helps them find "the good life" in a personal maturing relationship with Jesus Christ. Textbook **6-2018—$1.75**/Leader's Guide **6-2930—95¢**

THE WAR WE CAN'T LOSE Henry Jacobsen presents The Revelation as God's guarantee that His omnipotent Son will one day reign over the earth. Textbook **6-2047—$1.25**/Leader's Guide **6-2936—95¢**

BORN TO GROW Larry Richards shows how to develop spiritual attitudes, new patterns of living, and a new awareness of God after conversion to Christ. Excellent for new Christians. Textbook **6-2708—$1.75**/Leader's Guide **6-2920—95¢**

THE MAN WHO SHOOK THE WORLD Biblically authentic biography of Paul, by John Pollock. Every detail of historical background is from the most accurate scholarship available and personal research in Bible lands. Textbook **6-2233—$2.50**/Leader's Guide **6-2903—95¢**

WHERE IN THE WORLD ARE THE JEWS TODAY? James and Marti Hefley take a look into the Jews' spiritual, national. and prophetic situations. Textbook **6-2700—$1.75**/Leader's Guide **6-2914—95¢**

WINNING WAYS Suggestions. by LeRoy Eims, on how to prepare for witnessing, approaches that can lead to witnessing, and how to witness so that people will listen. Textbook **6-2707—$1.75**/Leader's Guide **6-2921—95¢**

WHAT EVERY CHRISTIAN SHOULD KNOW ABOUT GROWING LeRoy Eims displays a contagious sincerity and love for the Lord as he leads new believers into patterns of healthy Christian growth and discipleship. Textbook **6-2727 —$1.95**/Leader's Guide **6-2947—95¢**

THE BIBLE AND TOMORROW'S NEWS Dr. Charles C. Ryrie takes a new look at prophecy with the daily newspaper in hand. A sound, sober, and trustworthy study. Textbook **6-2017—$1.75**/Leader's Guide **6-2932—95¢**

WHAT DID JESUS SAY ABOUT THAT? Stanley C. Baldwin examines *all* Jesus said on 13 important subjects. Deals in depth with a search into their profound implications. Comprehensive. contemporary, and provocative. Leader's Guide includes overhead projector masters, with instructions for making transparencies. Textbook **6-2718—$1.95**/Leader's Guide **6-2939—$1.95**

> Add 40¢ postage and handling for the first book, and 10¢ for each additional title. Add $1 for minimum order service charge for orders less than $5.

VICTOR BOOKS

Buy these titles at your local Christian bookstore or order from   a division of SP Publications, Inc.

WHEATON ILLINOIS 60187